JESUS AND HIS FRIENDS

JESUS AND HIS FRIENDS

An exposition of John 14 – 17

D.A. Carson

Authentic

This edition first published 2010 by Authentic Media Limited
Milton Keynes
www.authenticmedia.co.uk

British Library Cataloguing-in-Publication Data

A catalogue record for this book is available from the
British Library

ISBN 978-1-85078-891-1

Cover design by Philip Miles
Printed and bound in Great Britain by
CPI Cox & Wyman, Reading, RG1 8EX

For David and Joyce Smith

Contents

Preface

For the last eight years I have spent more time studying the Gospel of John than any other part of the Scripture. This has proved to be a lesson in humility. John is simple enough for a child to read and complex enough to tax the mental powers of the greatest minds. As one commentator has put it, this book is like a pool in which a child may wade and an elephant may swim. I am not an elephant; but I have become aware of the many places where I am beyond my depth.

Up to now, what I have written on this Gospel was prepared for the well-trained minister or serious student, and is available only in journals or in books not likely to be read by the general reader. I am more and more convinced, however, that those of us who by the grace of God have been privileged to spend much time studying the Scriptures owe the fruit of our labours not only to the scholarly community but also to the church at large. A need exists for both academic and popular approaches; but this volume belongs to the latter camp. It grew out of a series of addresses given at several conferences in Canada and the United States. These have been worked over and rewritten as essays, a form more

congenial to the printed page than is a sermon; but I
have purposely refrained from obliterating all traces of
the earlier form.

It is common in the scholarly community to assert
that the historical Jesus was responsible for very little of
the teaching recorded in John 14 to 17. It will quickly
become obvious that I am not so sceptical. With some
hesitation I have refrained from adding an appendix to
explain my approach to historical-critical questions (as I
did in *The Sermon on the Mount: An Evangelical Exposition
of Matthew 5 to 7*, published by Authentic Media Limited); and only rarely have I alluded to questions of
authenticity in the course of the exposition. Those interested in knowing how I would approach such problems
may read 'Current Source Criticism of the Fourth
Gospel: Some Methodological Questions', in *Journal of
Biblical Literature* 97 (1978) 411–429, and 'Historical
Tradition in the Fourth Gospel: After Dodd, What?' in
Gospel Perspectives, vol. 2, ed. D. Wenham (1981).

Renae Grams and Karen Sich prepared the typescript
with their characteristic accuracy, efficiency and cheer-
fulness; and I am very grateful.

I pray that these short studies will be as spiritually
profitable to those who read them as they have been to
me as I prepared them. But above all, I pray that this volume will encourage many to return again and again to
the Scriptures themselves. Whatever helps us better
understand, obey and believe the Word of God con-
tributes to our eternal well-being; but the ultimate
source of that well-being is God alone.

Soli Deo Gloria.

D.A. Carson

1 (John 13)

Prologue

The atmosphere in the large upstairs room was tense, unhappy, uncertain.

The evening had gone badly from the start. The disciples had gathered with Jesus, as arranged, and climbed to the upstairs room where the food was already prepared. They looked around for the traditional servant to wash their feet; but seeing no-one, and being too polite to mention it, they stretched out on their pallets around the low eating table without saying a word. Jesus offered the traditional prayer of thanksgiving; and then they noticed that Jesus was pushing himself off his pallet. The talk was stilled. The Master quietly took off his cloak. To their utter consternation, he went over to the washstand, wrapped the towel around his waist, picked up the large basin of water, and headed for the nearest disciple.

Teachers shouldn't do things like that. Not even equals should wash one another's feet: it is a job for servants – and the servants with least seniority, at that. The first disciple, too surprised to move, too embarrassed to protest, felt his sandals being slipped off, and then the cool water and the dry towel. The Master proceeded to the second disciple, and to the third; all the while the silence was deafening.

Typically, it was Simon Peter who broke the silence. As Jesus approached to wash his feet, Peter curled up his legs, and pointed out the inappropriateness of the Master's action with what he thought was a tactful question: 'Lord, are you going to wash my feet?'

Jesus straightened his back, looked him straight in the eye and replied quietly, 'You do not realize now what I am doing, but later you will understand.'

Peter's voice hardened; someone had to speak out. If the Master could not see that he was demeaning himself, Peter would have to tell him. 'No,' he said, 'you'll never wash my feet.'

Still Jesus looked at him with that unwavering gaze. 'Unless I wash you,' he said, 'you have no part with me.'

Open confrontation. For a moment the still air was charged with suspense. Did Jesus not recognize that Peter was speaking out of love? But faced with a response like that, Peter was not slow in rising to the occasion. He decided to take advantage of the situation and declare his love in a different way. 'Then, Lord,' he replied, 'not just my feet but my hands and my head as well!'

That might have relieved the tension; but then Jesus added something more, something which, at the time, was highly enigmatic and restored the gloomy foreboding in the room. He said, 'A person who has had a bath needs only to wash his feet; his whole body is clean. And', he added, looking around the room, 'you are clean, though not every one of you.' And in the utter silence that followed, he finished washing their feet.

The disciples watched Jesus wipe his hands, don his cloak and return to his pallet. Unable to look at each other, embarrassed both for themselves and for their

Teacher, they were quietly grateful that the episode was over. And then all of a sudden it was not; for Jesus began speaking again.

'Do you understand what I have done for you?' he asked.

They understood well enough; he had washed their feet. But then they began to see that he expected a deeper answer than that. What Jesus had done for them was to provide a model; and as this truth slowly dawned on them, drawn out by the quiet question, they found their groping answers confirmed as Jesus responded to his own question.

'You call me "Teacher" and "Lord",' he said, 'and rightly so, for that is what I am. Now that I, your Lord and Teacher, have washed your feet, you also should wash one another's feet. I have set you an example that you should do as I have done for you. I tell you the truth, no servant is greater than his master, nor is a messenger greater than the one who sent him. Now that you know these things, you will be blessed if you do them.'

That was the first embarrassing episode of the evening. Jesus had talked on in vague terms about betrayal and other gloomy subjects; but at the time what he was saying did not seem too coherent. Conversation gradually resumed, and the feast began. Strangely, as the atmosphere improved, Jesus seemed to become more and more despondent, deeply troubled in spirit. Conversation drooped. Encouraged by the lull, Jesus spoke again, this time plainly.

'I tell you the truth,' he said, 'one of you is going to betray me.'

The atmosphere instantly became stultifying again. The silence returned, an engulfing blanket, as the disciples stared at each other. This time there was no doubt what the Master meant. The only question was which disciple Jesus had in mind. The stares around the low table were mixed: some curious, some blank, some frightened. Eating came to a standstill.

In a burst of confused questions, several asked incredulously if the Lord had them in mind; and Judas Iscariot joined in their number.

Peter recovered first; but remembering how his last outburst earned him a rather sharp rebuke, he was loath to plunge ahead with the obvious question. He caught John's eye and mouthed the question now gathering in everyone's mind. 'Ask him which one he means,' he mimed, nodding towards John who lay on the pallet next to Jesus.

John, leaning on his left arm, slowly twisted backward so that he could talk to Jesus. John's head fell back on Jesus' breast; and then John asked quietly, 'Lord, who is it?'

Jesus answered, 'It is the one to whom I will give this piece of bread when I have dipped it in the dish.'

Everyone stared at Jesus. No-one spoke. Slowly Jesus dipped his bread in the dish, shook off the excess and held the bread out to Judas Iscariot.

Now everyone stared at Judas. It did not seem possible that he could be a traitor. Had he not been with them from the beginning, preaching and performing miracles with the best of them? Had he not been trusted and respected enough to serve as treasurer? It was hard to believe that Judas could become a turncoat. When would this happen? Or was Jesus simply offering a warning, and hoping that a dangerous tendency could be nipped in the bud by a slicing thrust, by public exposure?

Still Jesus held out the bread to Judas. Judas felt the stares. Shamed and sullen, he said nothing while his racing mind searched out what he should do next. He had already made arrangements to betray Jesus; and now he had to come to a final decision. He had found the foot-washing episode so humiliating, so unfitting for any would-be Messiah, that he had found his decision to betray Jesus greatly reinforced. And now this! The temerity of this Jesus! But what was Jesus up to? Was he warning him? Or pleading with him to refuse to take the bread? Or calling his bluff? Or trying to shame him out of it? Just look at the stunned and stupid stares of these people – they can't seem to recognize that their vitality and independence are being emasculated by this Teacher who is curiously captivating, yet too meek and too weak to provide the leadership the nation needs.

Firmly, decisively, Judas reached out and took the dipped bread. The challenge was accepted, or the bluff called. Judas crossed some personal Rubicon, and Satan took hold of him.

Then Jesus spoke again, addressing Judas directly: 'What you are about to do, do quickly.' Judas answered with stony silence; but he pushed himself off his pallet and slowly rose to his feet. The others looked on, stunned, uncertain. It did not occur to them that Jesus was actually telling Judas to get on with the betrayal, to betray him quickly: for what sane man would say that? They could not imagine such a thing, because they still could not believe their Master was willingly and steadfastly taking all the steps that would lead to his own grim execution. Unable at this point to grasp the necessity of the cross in the plan of God, and Jesus' voluntary submission to that plan, they had no mental category in which they could place Jesus' comments, or by which they could make sense of Jesus' charge to Judas. Perhaps, they speculated, Jesus was moving on to some new subject. Perhaps Jesus was satisfied with the warning he had given, and was now showing Judas that in some sense he still trusted him to discharge his responsibilities as treasurer. It really was not very clear.

Judas opened the door and walked out; and it was night. Not till much later would John remember that blackness through the open door, and judge it fitting. The true light that gives light to every man had come into the world (1:9); but those who do evil hate the light and will not come into the light for fear their deeds may be exposed (3:20). Jesus claimed to be the light of the world (9:5): how appropriate that the betrayer of the light should walk out into the darkness.

No sooner had Judas gone than Jesus began to speak to the remaining disciples of his own departure. He spoke somewhat enigmatically in terms of being glorified, in terms of leaving them behind. He reminded them to love one another, and spoke consolingly about their future witness.

But most of what he said was puzzling. It was impressive in a way, and dramatic; but it was not very comprehensible. What the disciples did understand, and what alarmed them, was this talk of Jesus' departure. Finally Peter could take it no longer. He wanted plain answers to plain questions, and he wanted them now. He phrased his question bluntly, and asked it firmly: 'Lord, where are you going?'

That was how the third embarrassing and distressing episode began that evening. Jesus would not be pushed; and he replied calmly but still enigmatically, 'Where I am going, you cannot follow now, but you will follow later.'

Peter responded with another question: 'Lord, why can't I follow you now?' Then, fearing that perhaps his own allegiance was being impugned, he protested vigorously, 'I will lay down my life for you.'

Jesus answered, 'Will you really lay down your life for me? I tell you the truth, before the cock crows, you will disown me three times!'

Embarrassment, grief and tension can all heighten the senses and imprint details indelibly on to one's memory. That incredible night was for ever vivid to the disciples, not least after the resurrection when they could put it into proper perspective and appreciate fully what had happened and what Jesus had said. That was the evening Jesus instituted the Lord's Supper; but its significance awaited the events of the next three days. The fullest implications of the foot-washing, too, became clear in retrospect. Then the disciples could better understand that Jesus' washing his disciples' feet provided not only a moral example (13:15) but also a sign of the redemption and purification he was about to accomplish on their behalf (13:10–11). He not only washed their feet with water; much more, by his mission that weekend he would wash them completely. Again, he himself was the 'living water' which quenches all thirst (4:10; 7:37), and he would provide the Spirit as a continuous fount of 'living water' within each believer (7:38).

That night Jesus took advantage of the disciples' heightened senses to discourse one last time on many themes. No doubt he returned to many of the same themes after his resurrection (cf. Acts 1:3); but to explain some of these things, even in enigmatic fashion, before the cross, would ultimately assure his disciples that he was not himself caught off guard. The cross was neither a mistake nor a second thought, but part of his mission – indeed, the central part. 'I have told you now before it happens,' he said, 'so that when it does happen you will believe' (14:29).

Perhaps one of the most amazing features of this 'Farewell Discourse', as it has come to be called, is its beginning. It is Jesus who is going to the agony of the cross; it is Jesus who is troubled in spirit. Yet on this night when of all nights it would have been appropriate for his disciples to encourage him and support him, we discover that they can see only their loss. Jesus therefore must encourage them. On the very night he is to taste death on their behalf, he speaks to their confused bewilderment, fickle faith, dim vision and self-absorption; and he says, 'Do not let your hearts be troubled . . .'

2 (John 14:1–14)

An Introduction to Triumphant Faith

'Do not let your hearts be troubled. Trust in God; trust also in me. In my Father's house are many rooms; if it were not so, I would have told you. I am going there to prepare a place for you. And if I go and prepare a place for you, I will come back and take you to be with me that you also may be where I am. You know the way to the place where I am going.'

Thomas said to him, 'Lord, we don't know where you are going, so how can we know the way?'

Jesus answered, 'I am the way and the truth and the life. No-one comes to the Father except through me. If you really knew me, you would know my Father as well. From now on, you do know him and have seen him.'

Philip said, 'Lord, show us the Father and that will be enough for us.'

Jesus answered: 'Don't you know me, Philip, even after I have been among you such a long time? Anyone who has seen me has seen the Father. How can you say, "Show us the Father"? Don't you believe that I am in the Father, and that the Father is in me? The words I say to you are not just my own. Rather, it is the Father, living in me, who is doing his work. Believe me when I say that I am in the Father and the Father is in me; or at least believe on the evidence of the miracles themselves. I tell you the truth, anyone who has faith in me will do what I have been doing. He will do even greater things than these, because I am going to the Father. And I will do whatever you ask in my name, so that the Son may bring glory to the Father. You may ask me for anything in my name, and I will do it.'

Against the background of the disciples' confusion and anxiety, Jesus talks about serene faith, about spiritual tranquillity: 'Do not let your hearts be troubled. Trust in God; trust also in me' (14:1). To demand untroubled hearts (14:1*a*) would be but cruel taunt or empty counsel, were it not that Jesus also teaches the only basis on which his people could ever accomplish such a feat: faith, faith in the Father and faith in Jesus himself (14:1*b*).

Whether the text should be translated 'Trust in God; trust also in me' or 'You trust in God; trust also in me' is in one sense incidental; for in either case Jesus is linking himself directly with God. Every first-century Jew knew it was his duty to trust God; but for a man to exhort others to trust in him in the same way that they should trust in God must be taken, now as then, as a claim to deity. For a man to say 'Trust in me' in so absolute a context is either sublime or ridiculous: there is no middle ground. A man who is only a man is not deserving of such trust, and must in time disappoint it; a man who is also God not only deserves such trust, but cannot possibly betray it.

On the basis of trust in God and in Jesus, the disciples are not to be troubled. Presupposed are both the sovereignty and the goodness of God and of Jesus. They have the power to accomplish what they will, and they have the welfare of the disciples at heart: otherwise they could not be thought trustworthy in so absolute a sense.

No doubt such an exhortation could be profitably applied to Christians in every age who face staggering anxieties and troubles. Elsewhere in the New Testament, Paul generalizes the exhortation when he writes, 'Do not be anxious about anything, but in everything, by prayer and petition, with thanksgiving, present your requests to God. And the peace of God, which transcends all understanding, will guard your hearts and your minds in Christ Jesus' (Phil. 4:6–7). In the context of the Farewell Discourse, however, Jesus' encouragement to the disciples is designed to meet a specific situation. Not only have the painful incidents of the Last Supper – the foot-washing, the departure of Judas, the prediction of Peter's cowardice – caused malaise in these men; worse, Jesus has specifically told them he is about to go away and leave them. 'My children,' he said, 'I will be with you only a little longer. You will look for me, and just as I told the Jews, so I tell you now: Where I am going, you cannot come' (13:33).

Unable to grasp that Jesus' departure from them is his return to the glory rightly his, by way of the cross and the tomb, the disciples wallow in their misery, fearing they are about to be abandoned. We, too, may sometimes slither around in the slough of despond and feel abandoned; but the situation in John 13 and 14 is unique. The sense of abandonment experienced by the disciples was prompted by an unrepeatable event in the history of redemption: the physical departure of Jesus Christ by way of the cross. Therefore, although the disciples needed the general exhortation to trust in God and to trust in Jesus, they needed something more: they needed further instruction, more detailed explanation of the significance of the events to take place. Even if they remained unable to absorb all the details until after that epochal weekend had passed, Jesus' words provided not only some immediate relief, but the framework that ultimately made sense of the most important events in all history.

In other words, the Farewell Discourse must not be treated simplistically, as nothing more than Christian comfort designed to console defeated saints. Rather, it is first and foremost an exposition of the significance of Jesus' 'going away' to his Father via the cross. It is elemental theology; *and only as such does it offer encouragement and consolation.* For troubled Christians there is little genuine comfort that is divorced from the significance of the events of that one weekend in Jerusalem and its environs almost two thousand years ago. This was especially true for those first believers, whose anguish was made particularly acute by the fact that they themselves participated in those events, and were engulfed by them. But modern believers, too, best discover renewed faith and fortitude, not by clinging to isolated spiritual aphorisms and evangelical clichés, but by returning to a deep understanding of the historical and redemptive structure of their faith.

Within this framework, Jesus provides some content for his followers to believe (14:2–7): he enunciates truths they must believe if their faith is to be triumphant, their spirits tranquil. Unfortunatly, the disciples grasp little of this, because they have already misjudged who Jesus is. The profound implications of the exhortation, 'Trust in God; *trust also in me* (14:1) have quite passed them by; and therefore Jesus must review some of his earlier teaching and provide a lesson for slow learners concerning who he really is (14:8–14).

Some truths to be believed (14:2–7)

Jesus lays out three truths that must surely be believed if the faith of his disciples is to prove triumphant:

1. Jesus is not simply going away; he is, rather, going away to his Father's spacious house – and that, to prepare a place for his followers. 'In my Father's house are many rooms; if it were not so, I would have told you. I am going there to prepare a place for you' (14:2).

The Authorized Version promises 'many mansions' rather than 'many rooms'; and no doubt the prospect of an eternal mansion is more appealing to many than the prospect of an eternal room. The word *mansion* has called forth quite a number of songs which picture eternal bliss in largely materialistic categories: 'I've got a mansion just over the hilltop,' we sing, scarcely able to restrain our imaginations from counting the valets at our beck and call. 'A tent or a cottage, why should I care?/They're building a palace for me over there.' Here we even manage to upgrade 'mansion' to 'palace'.

The word used in the original text is an extremely rare one; but it is used in one other place in the New Testament – in this chapter, 14:23. There we learn that the Father and the Son, by means of the Holy Spirit, will make their 'abode' (AV) or 'dwelling' in the believer. The New International Version (hereafter cited NIV) puts it nicely, 'we will come . . . and *make our home* with him.' The word in question should not call forth images of a lush country estate. It is a neutral term, signifying a dwelling, an abode, a place to live. Certainly it would be a very strained metaphor which speaks of many mansions in a house.

Contextually, it is obvious that the disciples are not concerned at this point with the wealth of their eternal inheritance. They are upset over the prospect of losing Jesus. The essence of his assurance to them is that although he is returning to his Father's house, he will one day be united with his disciples again. The return to his Father's house is not a retreat into splendid isolation, but a journey to prepare a place for his followers. 'If it were not so,' he rebukes them gently, 'I would have told you' – as if to say only a gross form of unbelief imagines that Jesus could abandon his followers at all. How dare they think that he could prove as fickle as they? His integrity is such that if his ultimate purpose had been to leave his followers on their own, he would have told them.

The truth of the matter is that Jesus had repeatedly spoken to his men of his departure; but like so much of what he taught, their mind-set prevented them from grasping what he was saying until after the events to which he referred. 'What if you see the Son of Man ascend to where he was before!' (6:62) he once asked. Even to the Pharisees he declared, 'I am with you for only a short time, and then I go to the one who sent me. You will look for me, but you will not find me; and where I am, you cannot come' (7:33–34; cf. also 8:21). That very evening, after Judas Iscariot had left the upstairs room, Jesus told his disciples, 'My children, I will be with you only a little longer. You will look for me, and just as I told the Jews, so I tell you now: Where I am going, you cannot come' (13:33). But now he assures them of something more: his departure is for the purpose of establishing for them permanent dwelling-places in the very presence of God. That is the truth about his leaving. If believed, their faith would triumph over their doubts and their troubled minds. Such faith would dispel the nagging suspicions that they were being abandoned. Indeed, how could men who had every reason to trust in Jesus as they trusted in God stoop to think that his departure was not for their ultimate good?

Even the expression 'my Father's house' is evocative of the presence of God. When he cleaned out the temple, Jesus used the same expression: 'Get these out of here! How dare you turn *my Father's house* into a market!' (2:16; cf. Lk. 2:49). There, however, 'my Father's house' referred to the temple. But was not the temple understood to be the place where men could enter the very presence of God by means of sacrifices offered to atone for sin? Foreseeing that the ultimate sacrifice was himself, Jesus once claimed that the true temple was nothing less than his own body (2:21). Similarly, although 'the Father's house' was an apt description of the temple for as long as the temple served as the focal point for the meeting between God and man, it could apply more fully to heaven, the home of God, the ultimate hope of God's people, the promise of the beatific vision. 'Rooms' in such a house signifies nothing less than the sheer delight of for ever dwelling in the unshielded radiance of the glory of God.

Christians must not lose sight of this long-range perspective. We live in a day when we are being reminded again and again of our *temporal* privileges and responsibilities as Christians: we enjoy abundant life now, and we must remember to help the poor, seek justice for all, insist on integrity and demonstrate it ourselves. Such reminders are important, precisely because it is possible in a superficial sense to be heavenly minded yet morally and socially useless. At the same time, Christians must avoid identifying the goals of the kingdom of God with political, economic or social goals; or, more accurately, such

identification must never be exclusive. Just as the kingdom of Jesus Christ is not of this world (18:36), so also is
it not restricted to this world. Our ultimate goal is not the
transformation of society, as valuable as that may be. Our
goal is pure worship in the unrestricted presence of God.

That perspective, and that perspective alone, is powerful enough to call forth our unqualified obedience.
Such an eternal vantage-point enables us to be more
useful in our society than we would be otherwise; for,
following an exalted Master, we learn something of
service while walking in self-denial that eschews personal empire-building. Empire-building is so common a
temptation for idealists that today's revolutionaries
commonly become tomorrow's tyrants. The Christian
has the potential to escape this snare, for his highest
goal transcends the merely temporal. He magnifies
integrity coupled with meekness because he recognizes
that such graces are gifts from the Master who exemplified men.

This perspective is presupposed by the text, though
not elaborated. The goal of living for ever with Jesus in
his Father's house is given to Jesus' first disciples; and it
is given to us, too. Our danger, not shared by them, is
that we may be so comfortable as we luxuriate in the
blessings God has already given us that we may lose the
taste for finer things. We stop caring very much that
Jesus may leave us – not, now, to go to the cross, but to
teach us our dependence. Worse, we may not enjoy any
keen anticipation of eternity; we may neglect to cry with
believers in every age, 'Come, Lord Jesus!' The *status quo*
is what is desirable, not the consummation.

The irony of our situation is that our love of our privileges has not, by and large, produced any more triumphant faith, any more spiritual serenity, than would
otherwise be the case. Quite the reverse: we have

fomented a neurotic generation of malcontents. In the same way that Jesus' first disciples needed to trust Jesus and believe that his departure was for their eternal good, so we today need to trust Jesus and believe that his now long-past departure is for our eternal good. In both cases, it is the long-range view that lends stability to faith.

The true basis of stable faith may be better understood after the next clause is examined. Jesus says, 'I am going there to prepare a place for you.' The underlying Greek text precedes these words with a causal 'for': that is, 'In my Father's house are many rooms (the next words, 'if not, I would have told you,' are parenthetical); *for* I am going there to prepare a place for you.' The 'are' in the first line, as is often the case in John's Gospel, is proleptic (anticipatory). We might render the thought: 'In my Father's house there will be many rooms; for I am going there to prepare a place for you.'

But what is Jesus actually preparing, and why is it taking him so long? The first few verses of this Gospel have already insisted that the pre-incarnate Word was God's agent in creation. If he could speak and worlds burst into being, why has it taken so long to prepare a few rooms?

The answer becomes obvious when we closely examine Jesus' words as John reports them: '*I am going there* to prepare a place for you.' In this Gospel, the descriptions of Jesus' departure – also called his going, his returning to his Father, his glorification, his being lifted up – all refer to one event: his return to his Father by way of the cross and the resurrection, with all the redemptive significance embraced by this return. In 14:2, therefore, Jesus is not saying, in effect, 'I am returning to my Father's house so that, after I get there, I'll be able to get the place ready for you'; but rather, 'I am returning to my Father's house in order that this very return, this redemptive journey, may be the means of preparing the place.' Elsewhere in the New Testament we read of the activity of the exalted Jesus: he is even now the mediatorial king through whom all of God's sovereignty is exercised (1 Cor. 15:24ff.), the high priest with the permanent priesthood who always lives to intercede for his people (Heb. 7:24–25). But such activity is probably not in view in John 14. Rather, Jesus' 'going' is itself designed to prepare a place for his followers, not least by preparing his followers for the place, as Augustine has finely put it.

The faith of those first believers was stable and strong in proportion as it rested in Jesus as in God, believing that Jesus' departure was a return to his Father's presence, a return which itself opened up the Father's house to them. The faith of believers at the start of the twenty-first century is as stable and strong in proportion as it rests in Jesus as in God, believing that Jesus' departure via the cross, now an event more than two thousand years in the past, was his triumphant return to the Father, and the means by which we too never need fear abandonment. We may exult that Jesus went away to prepare a place for us, and this long-range perspective, this prospect of eternal joy, swallows up our transient fears in the serenity of faith. We exult with Paul, 'He who did not spare his own Son, but gave him up for us all – how will he not also, along with him, graciously give us all things?' (Rom. 8:32).

There is a second truth which helps to establish triumphant faith:

2. *Jesus is coming back for his own.* He promises, 'And if I go and prepare a place for you, I will come back and take you to be with me that you also may be where I am' (14:3).

This verse has called for several mutually exclusive interpretations. Because Jesus' 'going away' is a reference to his death, some argue that his promise 'I will come back' is a reference to his resurrection. This interpretation falters on two grounds: first, Jesus' 'going away' *includes* a reference to his death, but is not restricted to that: ultimately he is going by way of death *to his Father* (17:13). Therefore it is not obvious that 'I will come back' must be narrowed down to the resurrection. Second, Jesus promises to come back *and take his disciples to be with him*. It is not obvious that any such thing followed the resurrection. For similar reasons it is not very satisfying to think that Jesus' coming again is simply his coming in the presence of the Holy Spirit (as later in 14:23).

Others have argued strongly that Jesus' coming back is a promise that he will return for his disciples when they die, and bear them away to be with him. This passage is often read at Christian funerals, and probably that is the comfort such reading is intended to convey. This interpretation is possible; but it is by no means persuasive. The text nowhere speaks of the death of the disciples, nor even hints at it. Nowhere in John's Gospel or in his Epistles is there any clear enunciation of this teaching; and therefore we have no assurance that this was the sort of thing which interested John and which he would have recorded or to which he would have alluded.

It is better to take the promise as a reference to the second coming: Jesus will return to fetch his own and take them to be with him. He is not only going away; he is coming back. This theme John does treat elsewhere, both explicitly (e.g. 21:22) and implicitly in references to resurrection, ultimate judgment, last day, and the like (e.g. 6:54; 11:24–25; 1 John 4:17).

This is more than some far-off hope. The intensely personal nature of the promise must be noticed: '*I am going* there to prepare a place *for you . . . I will come back* and take *you* to be *with me* that *you also* may be where *I am*.' It is the sense of being abandoned that troubles the disciples; and Jesus replies that his departure is necessary preparation for his disciples to join him. And even further, he is coming back for them. They could not think of losing him; and he assures them that they are not losing him – they are gaining him.

The supreme hope of the church has always been the return of Jesus Christ. But in contemplating that happy prospect, we must never lose sight of the fact that the goal is to be *with Christ*. It is true that the second advent promises an end to history as we know it, and constitutes a guarantee that moral chaos and human rebellion shall not ultimately prevail. It is true that we are thereby reassured that history is neither out of control nor meaningless. But one must not neglect the greatest source of comfort of all: the prospect of being *with Christ*. Small wonder Jesus places such emphasis on the personal implications of his return. The consummation itself would be an empty triumph if Jesus were not there.

> All earth's flowing pleasures
> Were a wintry sea,
> Heav'n itself without Thee
> Dark as night would be.
>
> Lamb of God! Thy glory
> Is the light above.
> Lamb of God! Thy glory
> Is the life of love.
>
> *D.A. McGregor (1847–95)*

Believers will become serene and stable in their faith when they trust Jesus as they trust God, and fix their attention, their aspirations, their values on Jesus' return, and the blessed prospect of enjoying his presence for ever.

3. Jesus' followers know the way to the place where he is going (14:4–7). This is the third truth that must be understood and grasped. Jesus says, 'You know the way to the place where I am going' (14:4). (This is to be preferred to the textual variant, reflected in the Authorized Version, 'And whither I go ye know, and the way ye know.') Jesus is saying something like this: By now, from all that I have told you, you surely know that the way to my Father's house is, for me, both the way of shame and crucifixion, and the way of glory and resurrection. I have repeatedly spoken of being 'lifted up', of being betrayed, of dying: so you must come to grips with the fact that although I now speak of going to my Father, I am going via the cross. That is the way to where I am going. This you know.

It is Thomas who asks the question; but probably others asked it in their minds: 'Lord, we don't know where you are going, so how can we know the way?' (14:5). In one sense there is something attractively straightforward about this man Thomas. We think of him as the doubter because of his rigid scepticism shortly after the resurrection (20:24–29); but even there, it is not altogether clear that any of the other disciples would have fared any better had they been absent and missed Jesus' first post-resurrection appearance to the gathered apostles. It is worth remembering that this same Thomas is prepared to face death with Jesus: 'Let us also go [to the Jerusalem area], that we may die with him' (11:16). He is a blunt man who faces fear, doubt and confusion head-on. He will not bluff, nor sport a pious face and nod wisely as if he understood what he does not understand. What he says, in effect, is this: Look, you tell us we know the way to where you're going. I'm telling you we don't even know where you're going; so how could we possibly know the way there?

Thomas's objection is even more ignorant than he thinks. Jesus has been talking about going to his Father and the way he himself must take in order to get there. Thomas claims he does not know where Jesus is going, nor the way – implying that the way Jesus takes to get wherever he is going will also be the way the disciples must take to follow him there. How can they know how to follow Jesus to his Father's house if they do not know the way there? Thus Thomas has failed to distinguish between the way Jesus must take to return to his Father, and the way the disciples must take to join him. This is the same sort of error Peter made a few minutes earlier when he asked impulsively, 'Lord, why can't I follow you now? I will lay down my life for you' (13:37). Quite the contrary: Jesus would lay down his life for Peter, and that redemptive act would open up the only way by which Peter would one day follow Jesus to the Father's presence.

Jesus, sensitive to Thomas's misunderstanding, stops talking about his own way to the Father, the way of the cross, and answers Thomas's question by telling him the way the disciples must travel: 'I am the way', he answers, 'and the truth and the life. Noone comes to the Father except through me' (14:6). In this fashion one of the greatest utterances in Holy Scripture is called forth from the Master by the inability of his disciples to grasp what he had been teaching.

It is an amazing statement. 'I am the way' – spoken by one whose way was the ignominious shame of a Roman cross, the death of despised and debased criminals. 'I am the truth' – spoken by one about to be condemned by lying witnesses, one who was generally not believed by his own people, by his own family. 'I am the life' – uttered by one whose battered corpse would shortly rest in a dark tomb, sealed up by the authorities.

There is glory in this paradox, and much room for adoring meditation. Because Jesus' own way was the cross, he himself became the way for others. As the Lamb of God, he took away the sin of the world (1:29); as the good shepherd, he laid down his life for the sheep (10:11). The lamb dies, the world lives. The shepherd dies, the sheep live. Jesus is the gate by which men enter and find life (10:9; cf. Heb. 10:19–20); he is their way. The way of Jesus is the cross; the way of the disciples is Jesus. Small wonder that early Christians were called followers of the Way (Acts 9:2; 22:4; 24:14).

He who was betrayed by an apostle, disowned by another apostle, abandoned by all the apostles, condemned through lying witnesses, was the truth. We do not read simply that what he *speaks* is true, but that he himself *is* the truth. He is the truth incarnate, just as he is love incarnate and holiness incarnate; for he is the Word incarnate. 'The Word became flesh and lived for a while among us. We have seen his glory, the glory of the one and only Son, who came from the Father, full of grace *and truth*' (1:14). 'For the law was given through Moses; grace *and truth* came through Jesus Christ. No-one has ever seen God, but God the only Son, who is at the Father's side, has made him known' (1:17–18). John is not telling us that Moses' writings were not true, nor that they were something other than God's Word. But however much the law was revealed by God, the law was not the unveiling of God himself, the revelation of grace and truth incarnate.

At the Christmas break in 1963, I brought home to the Ottawa area a friend I had come to know and enjoy at the university I was attending. Mohammed Yousuf Guraya was a Pakistani, a devout Muslim, a gentle and sensitive friend. He was trying to win me to Islam; I was trying to win him to Christ. He had started to read the Gospel of John when I took him to visit the Parliament Buildings in Ottawa. We enjoyed a guided tour of those majestic structures and learnt something of their history and symbolism. Our group had reached the final foyer when the guide explained the significance of the stone figurines sculpted into the fluted arches. One he pointed to represented Moses, designed to proclaim that government turns on law.

'Where is Jesus Christ?' Guraya asked with his loud, pleasant voice, his white teeth flashing a brilliant smile behind his black beard.

'I don't understand,' the guide stammered.

'Where is Jesus Christ?' Guraya pressed, a trifle more slowly, a little more loudly, enunciating each word for fear his accent had rendered his question incomprehensible.

The tourists in our group appeared to be embarrassed. I simultaneously chortled inwardly, wondering what was coming next, and wondered if I should intervene or keep my counsel.

'I don't understand,' the guide repeated, somewhat baffled, somewhat sullen, 'What do you mean? Why should Jesus be represented here?'

Guraya replied, somewhat astonished himself now: 'I read in your Holy Book that the law was given by Moses, but grace and truth came through Jesus Christ. *Where is Jesus Christ?*'

I think my friend Guraya had felt the impact of John's Gospel more deeply than I had. It is in line with the framework of John's prologue (1:1–18), where the eternal Word becomes the incarnate Word, that Jesus himself claims, 'I am the truth.'

'I am the life.' Earlier, at the tomb of Lazarus, Jesus declared, 'I am the resurrection and the life. He who believes in me will live, even though he dies; and whoever lives and believes in me will never die' (11:25–26). Of Jesus, John writes, 'He is the true God and eternal life' (1 John 5:20). He who died, condemned, enables others to live, forgiven.

> I am the way to God; I did not come
> To light a path, to blaze a trail, that you
> May simply follow in my tracks, pursue
> My shadow like a prize that's cheaply won.
> My life reveals the life of God, the sum
> Of all he is and does. So how can you,
> The sons of night, look on me and construe
> My way as just the road for you to run?
>   My path takes in Gethsemane, the Cross,
>   And stark rejection draped in agony.
>   My way to God embraces utmost loss:
>   Your way to God is not my way, but me.
> Each other path is dismal swamp, or fraud.
> I stand alone: I am the way to God.
>
> I am the truth of God: I do not claim
> I merely speak the truth, as though I were
> A prophet (but no more), a channel, stirred
> By Spirit power, of purely human frame.
> Nor do I say that when I take his Name
> Upon my lips, my teaching cannot err
> (Though that is true). A mere interpreter
> I'm not, some prophet-voice of special fame.
>
>   In timeless reaches of eternity
>   The Triune God decided that the Word,

The self-expression of the Deity,
　Would put on flesh and blood – and thus be heard.
The claim to speak the truth good men applaud.
I claim much more: I am the truth of God.

I am the resurrection life. It's not
As though I merely bear life-giving drink,
A magic elixir which (men might think)
Is cheap because though lavish it's not bought.
The price of life was fully paid: I fought
With death and black despair; for I'm the drink
Of life. The resurrection morn's the link
Between my death and endless life long sought.
　I am the firstborn from the dead; and by
　My triumph, I deal death to lusts and hates.
　My life I now extend to men, and ply
　Them with the draught that ever satiates.
Religion's page with empty boasts is rife:
But I'm the resurrection and the life.

The triple claim is staggering. The articles are not accidental: 'I am *the* way and *the* truth and *the* life'; he is not
some pleasant alternative, a way among others. Lest the
point should be missed, the second part of the verse
drives it home: 'No-one comes to the Father except
through me.'

This last clause accomplishes two things. First, by
speaking plainly of going to the Father through himself,
Jesus points out how Thomas has entirely misunder-
stood the earlier comments he made about his own way
to the Father. Thomas and other followers must recognize that the way Jesus takes is not simply to be imitated.
To join Jesus in the Father's house demands the recognition that *Jesus himself is* the way. Jesus' followers must not
simply follow his true teaching or copy his life: rather,

they recognize in him the truth incarnate, worship him, and receive life from him. 'No-one comes to the Father except *through me.*'

Not less significant is the second thing on which this statement insists. Jesus is the *exclusive* way, truth and life. This is not popular in our syncretistic age; but the same idea is taught repeatedly in the New Testament. 'Salvation is found in no-one else,' proclaims Peter, 'for there is no other name under heaven given to men by which we must be saved' (Acts 4:12). Adds Paul, 'But even if we or an angel from heaven should preach a gospel other than the one we preached to you, let him be eternally condemned!' (Gal. 1:8). Perhaps it is particularly important to recognize this exclusive strain in John's Gospel, because here, more than in many books of the New Testament, there is a wide use of literary and religious terminology found in other religions. John may be prepared to borrow the religious vocabulary of others; but he is not prepared to concede that salvation is found in any other than Jesus. And this, he insists, is the teaching of Jesus himself.

This is the answer to Thomas's question. Jesus no longer focuses on the way he himself must go; he focuses rather on the way the disciples must go. The misunderstanding of Thomas and his colleagues turns on their failure to perceive who Jesus really is, and the nature of the mission he has set out to perform. Therefore Jesus goes on to say, 'If you really knew me, you would know my Father as well' (14:7).

This verse (14:7) has a textual complication that is extremely difficult to resolve. The text behind the NIV reads: 'If you really knew me, you would know my Father as well. From now on, you do know him and have seen him.' This suggests a rebuke: If you really knew me, as by now you certainly should, you would know my

Father as well. The other main textual evidence supports
the NIV footnote to verse 7: 'If you really have known me,
you will know my Father as well. From now on, you do
know him and have seen him.' This suggests a promise:
If you have now come to know me, as you have done,
you will know my Father as well. Some have argued that
the second part of the verse, 'From now on, you do know
him and have seen him,' forces the second reading. On
the contrary: Philip goes on to show that they still do not
really know him (14:8). The second part of 14:7 is saying
that at one level the disciples have indeed come to know
Christ: they could describe him, talk with him, travel
with him, eat with him, ask him questions, and the like.
On this basis, because Jesus and his Father are one
(10:30), they have, objectively speaking, come to know
the Father as well. Because of who Jesus is, to know Jesus
is to know God. That is objectively so. The irony is that
the disciples themselves do not perceive what they have
come to know! They know Jesus; but, failing even yet to
grasp who he really is, they do not really know him and
thus recognize that to know him is to know God.

It seems best, on balance, to recognize that Jesus is rebuking them for their slowness in coming to perceive who he
is. Unlike the Pharisees (8:19) the disciples have come some
way in knowing Jesus; but they should have come further.
He identities himself again as the one who has made God
manifest (cf. 1:18): 'From now on, you do know him and
have seen him' (14:7). The disciples must see that their
knowledge of Jesus is nothing less than knowledge of God;
for Jesus himself is the way, the truth and the life. To see this
truth clearly is then the equivalent of truly knowing Jesus.
Thus, Jesus' followers do indeed know the way to the place
where Jesus is going (14:4); for they know Jesus. The problem is that they do not themselves perceive that they know
the way: in that sense they do not know him.

The issue is profoundly Christological. This third truth, which Jesus' disciples must firmly grasp if their faith is to be triumphant, is *who Jesus is*. Really to know who Jesus is, is to know the way they must take to reach the place Jesus is going. We have thus returned to the challenge of the first verse, where Jesus says, 'Do not let your hearts be troubled. Trust in God; *trust also in me.'* Stable, serene faith must have as its object Jesus himself.

Jesus' comfort to his disciples has become intensely Christological; but his disciples are still unable to absorb these sublime truths. Jesus finds it necessary to summarize some of what he has long taught, and explain more fully the profound Christological claim he has made.

A lesson for slow learners: a summary exposition of the revelation of the Father in the Son (14:8–14)

As a teacher, I am greatly encouraged that Jesus himself had slow learners. As one of Jesus' slowest learners, I am more grateful yet. My slow learners are more often slow because of limited capacity than because of laziness or perversity; but Jesus' slow learners are more often slow because of morally indefensible unbelief and even disobedience than for more flattering reasons.

Despite the clarity of Jesus' claim, the apostles cannot accept it at face value. Steeped in Jewish heritage in which monotheism played so strong a part, they could scarcely conceive of a trinitarian monotheism like that which Christians came in time to confess. They were still maintaining a fundamental chasm between Jesus and the Father. Sad to tell, some of Jesus' most bitter opponents discerned what Jesus was claiming more swiftly than did his apostles. We seek to stone you, they said, 'for blasphemy,

because you, a mere man, claim to be God' (10:33). But at
this late date, Philip can still ask, 'Lord, show us the Father
and that will be enough for us' (14:8).

Jesus answered, 'Don't you know me, Philip, even
after I have been among you such a long time? Anyone
who has seen me has seen the Father. How can you say,
"Show us the Father"?' (14:9). In effect, Jesus tells Philip
that his question is otiose precisely because the Father
has made himself known in the Word, who is God, but
who has become flesh. Therefore whoever has seen the
incarnate Word has seen the Father. Had not Jesus
already made this clear? Not long before he had publicly
taught, 'When a man believes in me, he does not believe
in me only, but in the one who sent me' (12:44).

But how can this be?

1. Statement of fact: the revelation of the Father in the Son.
'Don't you believe that I am in the Father, and that the
Father is in me? The words I say to you are not just my
own. Rather, it is the Father, living in me, who is doing
his work' (14:10).

To understand this verse adequately, it is necessary to
back off from it a little and to reflect on John's presentation of Jesus Christ in the fourth Gospel,[1] and also on the
way Christians have struggled to formulate theological
statements about the deity and humanity of Jesus Christ
while still remaining true to the biblical givens.

Many people are aware that John's Gospel greatly
stresses Jesus' deity. He is identified with the Word
incarnate; and from all eternity that Word was God (1:1).
In a moment of high drama, Thomas worships the resurrected Jesus in terms rightly applicable to God alone:
'My Lord and my God!' (20:28); and Jesus accepts this
ascription of deity and pronounces a blessing on those

who come to similar faith without requiring similar proof (20:29). The attributes of deity are applied to Jesus, and so also are the functions of the deity. Small wonder Jesus says to Philip, 'Anyone who has seen me has seen the Father' (14:9).

But there is another emphasis in John's Gospel which many overlook: Jesus' obedience to and utter dependence upon his Father. Jesus' role is to do the will of the one who sent him, and to finish his work (4:34). 'I tell you the truth,' Jesus insists, 'the Son can do nothing by himself; he can do only what he sees his Father doing . . . By myself I can do nothing; I judge only as I hear, and my judgment is just, for I seek not to please myself but him who sent me' (5:19,30). Again: 'My teaching is not my own. It comes from him who sent me' (7:16). If the Father who sent Jesus has not abandoned him, it is because, in Jesus' words, 'I always do what pleases him' (8:29). Even Jesus' sacrifice of himself, as the good shepherd for his sheep, is an action taken in response to his Father's 'command' (10:18). Towards the end of his public ministry, Jesus could claim, 'I did not speak of my own accord, but the Father who sent me commanded me what to say and how to say it . . . So whatever I say is just what the Father has told me to say' (12:49–50). And in the prayer he utters just before the cross, Jesus can claim, 'I have brought you glory on earth by completing the work you gave me to do' (17:4).

What shall we make of these seemingly opposed themes? Christians hold that Jesus is truly God and truly man; but it is somewhat astonishing to observe in detail the biblical contours of this amazing doctrine. In John's Gospel, Jesus is one with God, with respect to man, in creation, revelation and authority; yet he is one with man, with respect to God, in submission, dependence and obedience.

Christians through the centuries have tried to offer formulations which do justice to all this apparently disparate biblical evidence.

They have pondered what the eternal Word would have had to give up in order to become the incarnate Word. To use the categories Paul employs in Philippians 2:5–11, they ask what Christ 'emptied himself' of in order to join the human race.

The right answer to such questions is not easy to find; but it is fairly easy to detect large batches of wrong answers. Some suggest that Christ gave up his deity in becoming a man; but that is surely too easy, since the New Testament insists that Jesus during his ministry and passion was both God and man. Others say that he gave up some of his divine attributes – perhaps his omniscience, his omnipotence, his omnipresence. The problem with such a formulation is that a being cannot readily be separated from his attributes. If I see a being which looks like a gorilla, runs like a gorilla, and has all the attributes of a gorilla, I assume I am seeing a gorilla. If the being is said to be a gorilla, but has only a few of a gorilla's attributes but many of the attributes of an arctic lemming, I am unlikely to be impressed by enthusiastic claims that the being is indeed a gorilla. When Paul, for instance, insists that 'in Christ all the fullness of the Deity lives in bodily form' (Col. 2:9), he seems to eliminate the possibility of an incarnation which retains only some attributes of deity; and Paul is not alone in this insistence.

Still other theologians have suggested that although the eternal Son of God did not abandon any of his divine attributes, he did abandon the *use* of his divine attributes. This would mean that Jesus Christ during his ministry never utilized more than what, say, an Old Testament prophet utilized. After all, if Jesus performed miracles, so did they. If Jesus claimed to speak the words of God, so did they. But even this restricted formulation fails. In all of the Gospels Jesus claims for himself a relationship with the Father that no mere prophet ever enjoyed. In all of the Gospels, but especially in John's Gospel, the miracles performed are construed as signs which point to who Jesus is. Outside John's Gospel, the hushing of the storm elicits fear and amazement and the pregnant question, 'Who is this? He commands even the winds and the water, and they obey him' (Lk. 8:25; cf. Mt. 14:33). And who can forgive sins, in any absolute sense, but God alone (cf. Mk. 2:1–12)?

Some, therefore, attempt a further refinement. The eternal Son of God, they say, for the purposes of the incarnation, abandoned the *independent* use of his divine prerogatives. This is very close to being right. The Son of God abandoned any use of his divine prerogatives and capabilities which, as a man, he would not have enjoyed, *unless his heavenly Father gave him direction to use such prerogatives.* He therefore would not use his powers to turn stones into bread for himself: that would have been to vitiate his identification with human beings and therefore to abandon his mission, for human beings do not have instant access to such solutions. His mission prohibited him from arrogating to himself the prerogatives rightly his. But if that mission required him to multiply loaves for the sake of the five thousand, he did so. Even his knowledge was self-confessedly limited (Mt. 24:36).

We are dealing with holy things, things which, despite our best efforts at analysis and formulation, still defy our finite capacities to understand – they prompt us to cover our mouths in silent worship. The Word was with God, and the Word was God: that is clearly a given. The Word became flesh: that too is a given. When we move outside the givens, we are in danger of introducing some new implication which the Scriptures elsewhere disown. Even in the last attempted formulation, there is a problem. To say that the eternal Son of God for the purposes of the incarnation abandoned the independent use of his divine prerogatives is almost to suggest that the pre-incarnate Christ enjoyed unrestricted independence in the use of his divine prerogatives. Then it becomes extremely difficult to imagine how one could still defend that form of monotheism which the doctrine of the Trinity represents. Was the Son ever independent of his Father's will? God *sent* his Son into the world; and even if we assume the Son willingly acquiesced in this mission, we always discover in what little we know of the Son's pre-incarnate relationships with his Father that the initiative and the command are with the Father while submission and obedience belong to the Son. Dare we therefore suppose that the Son *ever* enjoyed a truly *independent* use of his divine prerogatives?

In one sense it is right to suppose that the Son, as a distinguishable and distinct person, possessed 'independence' as a person; but it would fly in the face of Scripture to think that such 'independence' could result in one course of action in the Son and a disparate course of action in the Father, or that their respective roles could be reversed. Can we say, then, that the formulation we have ventured is acceptable?

I do not think it is; not, at least, if the word *independent* is stressed and made absolute. But perhaps we are very close to the best theological formulation, however inadequate it may be to describe a reality as sublime as the incarnation, if we willingly force the formulation into less precise moulds. If we say that the eternal Son for the purposes of the incarnation abandoned some substantial measure of independence in the use of his divine prerogatives, we are less than perspicuous, but probably we more truly reflect the biblical givens.

John sees the loss that the Word faced in becoming flesh as a loss in glory. That is why he records the content of Jesus' final sustained prayer before the cross: 'And now, Father, glorify me in your presence with the glory I had with you before the world began' (17:5). Such a summary statement is about as far as we can go; but it is not very far, if only because *glory* and *glorify* are powerful words which call up mighty images but do not convey precise information. What is clear is that the pre-incarnate Son and the post-ascension Son enjoy the same glory as the Father; but on his earthly mission the Son laid his glory aside.

We are now in a better place to think again about the passages in John's Gospel which stress Jesus' dependence upon and submission to his Father. Jesus not only says, 'I tell you the truth, the Son can do nothing by himself; he can do only what he sees his Father doing'; but then he adds, *'because whatever the Father does the Son also does'* (5:19). Jesus is so utterly dependent on his Father's direction that *whatever* he says or does is nothing less and nothing other than what his Father says and does. 'Whatever I say', he claims, 'is just what the Father has told me to say' (12:50). In fact, most of the passages which mark Jesus' dependence and 'sentness' function in their contexts as the ground of Jesus' authority (5:17–18,19–30; 6:29,32–33; 7:16,18,28–29; 8:16,29,42; 10:17–18; 11:41–42; 12:45,48,50; 14:23–24,28–31; 17:2,7).

This is the magnificence of the irony: as a man, Jesus is utterly dependent upon God; but that dependence is so absolute, so unalloyed, that in reality all he says and does is exactly what God says and does and therefore has all God's authority behind it. The absoluteness of the self-denial has issued in the absoluteness of the

authority; but this authority is now vested in an incarnate person, a human being who can be immediately
perceived and touched and heard by other human
brings. In speaking God's words (3:34; 7:16; 8:26,38,40;
14:10,24; 17:8), performing only the Father's works
(4:34; 5:17,19ff.,30,36; 8:28; 14:10; 17:4,14) and doing
only the Father's will (4:34; 5:30; 6:38; 10:25,37), Jesus
stands in perfect submission to his Father, and simultaneously stands with his Father in perfect authority over
men.

Because of this unique stance in one person, the Lord
Jesus Christ, it follows that the man who accepts *Jesus'*
testimony has certified that *God* is truthful (3:33). True
faith that has eternal life hears *Jesus'* word and believes
the one who sent him (5:24; cf. 14:24). Only Jesus has seen
the Father (6:46); but now the one who has seen Jesus
has seen the Father (14:9), And if all this brings glory to
the Father (does not Jesus pray, 'I have brought you
glory on earth by completing the work you gave me to
do' [17:4]?), it is likewise the divine method of ensuring
that all men honour the Son just as they honour the
Father (5:23): 'He who does not honour the Son does not
honour the Father, who sent him.'

We are now better situated to understand John 14:10:
'Don't you believe that I am in the Father, and that the
Father is in me? The words I say to you are not just my
own [the Greek is stronger yet: *The words I say to you I do
not speak of myself*]. Rather, it is the Father, living in me,
who is doing his work.'

Jesus here provides his disciples with yet another
summary statement of his relationship with his Father,
something he has been teaching them all along. He is
insisting that his words and works are the words and
works of the Father, and thereby his Father has

revealed himself in his Son. What they have been witnessing these past years as they lived and travelled
with Jesus is nothing less than the revelation of the
Father in the Son.

Analogies do not help a great deal. Preachers have
often likened the incarnation to the decision of a great
and autocratic king to don peasant garb and visit his
subjects on their terms, incognito, refusing to use his
regal authority to call for help or protection when he
might need it. But the analogy, by illuminating the mission of the Son, clouds the relationship of the Son to his
Father. Who is back home at the king's castle? Analogies
fail us; for who or what is closely analogous to God or to
the incarnation of the Son whom he loves? To reflect biblical truth on these matters, we must insist that the Son
is ontologically God, divine in his very being; yet in his
mission as a man, he most reflects God by hiding his
own glory and, in perfect response to his Father, by
showing forth by his words and deeds his Father's glory.
The revelation of the Father in the Son is the essential
background to the drama of redemption about to unfold
in Jerusalem, on the Mount of Olives, at Golgotha, and
in an empty tomb.

This is a momentous claim. The disciples are still asking to see the Father, when all along they have been
enjoying the brightest possible revelation of the Father
without recognizing it. So blind are the spiritual eyes of
man that he cannot by himself see light in its brilliance.
So slow is the mind of man in thinking over spiritual
things that he stumbles over central truths that have
been taught again and again.

If Jesus' disciples more surely grasp that he is himself
the revelation of the Father, his comforting words will
have greater effect: 'Do not let your hearts be troubled.
Trust in God; trust also in me' (14:1).

2. Exhortation to believe the fact of the revelation of the Father in the Son. Jesus goes on to encourage his disciples: 'Believe me when I say that I am in the Father and the Father is in me; or at least believe on the evidence of the miracles themselves' (14:11).

The belief the disciples ought to vest in Jesus is neither *merely* personal nor void of content. Their belief is to be personal in that it is belief in Jesus himself; but such belief in Jesus himself entails believing that the things Jesus says are true: 'Believe *me* when I *say that* . . .' Belief in the person of Jesus should evoke belief in the truth of the content of what he teaches. In this instance the content of what he teaches has to do with his person, with who he is. This means that believing in the truth of what he teaches will therefore affect one's belief in Jesus as a person. The argument is in a circle, but the circle is not vicious.

It is sad that Jesus finds it necessary to exhort the followers closest to him to believe his words, and therefore to believe that he is himself the revelation of the Father. Sad, indeed; but not strange. Is not our own unbelief proof enough of the commonness of unbelief? Even after we have been assured of God's love for us again and again, of his sovereign pleasure to bless his people with what he judges good for them, do we not retreat to practical scepticism when difficult circumstances seem to call in question his goodness or his power?

Jesus' first disciples in John 14 are experiencing difficulties of several kinds. They are perhaps intellectually slow to believe the daring claim on Jesus' lips, made repeatedly, that he is in the Father and the Father in him. Worse, they are bound up emotionally as well as intellectually as they wrestle with talk about death, betrayal, Jesus' departure, their inability to follow him at present, and the like. What they need more than anything else is *to believe Jesus, to believe that what he is saying is true.* If only they believe, then the uncertainties surrounding these other large matters will be swallowed up by confidence that Jesus is none other than the revelation of the Father. There is no belief more basic to spiritual triumph than that.

Perceiving their continued unbelief, Jesus goes one step further. 'At least believe on the evidence of the miracles themselves' (14:11). Jesus is under no illusions about the power of his miracles to call forth faith. He is aware that after the stupendous miracle of the raising of Lazarus, though many Jews were encouraged to put their faith in him, the same act provoked others to inform on him to the religious authorities (11:45–46) – who in turn expanded their plot to kill Jesus to include killing Lazarus as well (12:10–11). (Their theory was: If the evidence is particularly compelling, get rid of the evidence.) Did not Jesus himself once say, 'If they do not listen to Moses and the Prophets, they will not be convinced even if someone rises from the dead' (Luke 16:31)? Jesus rebukes those who do not believe unless they see miraculous signs and wonders (4:48); and elsewhere he teaches that miracles by themselves do not prove that the person performing them is good or true (Matt. 24:24); for miracles may be done by false Christs and false prophets. It is always extremely dangerous to identify every manifestation of the supernatural with the divine – a lesson desperately needed by the modern generation.

But to admit that signs and wonders do not necessarily command belief, or to note that they may induce false belief, is not to say that they have no evidential value at all, nor that they cannot be adduced to deepen faith. To his opponents, Jesus says, 'even though you do not believe

me, believe the miracles, that you may learn and understand that the Father is in me, and I in the Father' (10:38).
The same challenge is now offered to the disciples.

We would do well to be less concerned with *how*
people come to deep faith, and more concerned *that the
faith be true* – true both subjectively (that there be genuine trust and commitment) and objectively (that the
object of the faith be true). Some come to put their trust
in Jesus because they are wooed by his love; others come
because they fear the threat of judgment. Some learn to
trust Christ because of the example of other Christians;
others come to faith reading the Scriptures on their own,
with no Christian witness anywhere near. Some come to
Christ because they are intellectually convinced of the
truth of his claims; others come because of the impact of
his miracles. Our sovereign, gracious God uses all of
these means and more; and we must not despise any of
them, nor elevate one to a position of exclusive
supremacy, nor think that any means is itself sufficient
to induce faith.

So Jesus, after briefly affirming afresh that he himself
is the revelation of the Father, encourages his followers
to believe this truth. But it must not be thought that such
faith is sterile, merely intellectual, rather arid.

*3. Results of believing the fact of the revelation of the Father
in the Son.* 'I tell you the truth, anyone who has faith in
me will do what I have been doing. He will do even
greater things than these, because I am going to the
Father. And I will do whatever you ask in my name, so
that the Son may bring glory to the Father. You may ask
me for anything in my name, and I will do it' (14:12–14).

The person who has true faith in Jesus Christ is promised two things.

First, such a person will do greater things than Jesus' works. But what does 'greater' mean? Shall Christians perform more sensational acts? It is difficult to imagine miracles more sensational than those of Jesus; 'greater' surely doesn't mean that. Might 'greater' mean 'more numerous' or 'more widely dispersed'? In that sense, Christians have indeed done 'greater' things than Jesus did. We have preached all around the world, seen millions of men and women converted, dispensed aid, education and food to still more millions. The 'greater' works may therefore be the gathering of converts into the church through the witness of the disciples (cf. 17:20; 20:29), and the overflow of kindness that stems from transformed lives.

Jesus says the greater works will take place 'because I am going to the Father'. In other words, Jesus' departure through death and resurrection to exaltation is the precondition of his disciples' mission. Because he 'goes to the Father', the church embarks on her mission. Moreover, Jesus' exaltation is the precondition of the descent of the promised Holy Spirit (7:39; 16;7) who will work with the disciples in their witness (15:26–27; cf. 16:7–11). For these reasons the followers of Jesus will perform 'greater' works.

But although this explanation is no doubt correct, why does Jesus speak of 'greater' works when this explanation sounds rather as if he meant 'more' works?

We may be helped by comparing a statement of Jesus in Matthew 11:11: 'I tell you the truth: Among those born of women there has not risen anyone *greater* than John the Baptist; yet he who is least in the kingdom of heaven is *greater* than he.' The point of the comparison is that, despite the Baptist's unequalled greatness, he never participated in the kingdom of heaven. His calling placed him too early in the history of redemption to permit such participation. In that sense, the least person privileged to participate in the kingdom is *greater* than John the Baptist. It is a greatness of privilege that is at stake, a greatness conferred with the privilege of participating in the already inaugurated eschatological age.

Something similar may be in view in John 14. Jesus, by his redemptive work, his 'going to the Father', inaugurates this new phase in the history of redemption; and the disciples in their mission participate in the works peculiar to this already-dawned eschatological age. Jesus in his earthly ministry never did. His work brought it about; but then he left and did not himself participate in it (in his bodily presence) after Pentecost. This does not mean that Jesus' disciples are greater than he is. It does mean that their works are greater than his in this respect, that they are privileged to participate in the effects of Jesus' completed work. Until he returned to his Father and bestowed the Holy Spirit, everything Jesus did was of necessity still incomplete. By contrast, the works of the disciples participate in the new situation that exists once Jesus' work is complete. Their works are greater in that they are privileged to take place after the moment of fulfilment.

This magnificent canvas must constantly be held before the eyes of every Christian witness. Our faith in Jesus does not thrust us into a struggle where we are alone, where the outcome is unsure, where the promised blessing is exclusively reserved for 'the sweet by and by'. Quite the contrary: our faith in Jesus thrusts us into a struggle in which the decisive battle has already been won, in which the promised eschatological blessing has already dawned even if it is not yet consummated. Indeed, our own feeble efforts participate in the triumph of Christ and the work of his bequeathed Spirit to call forth an innumerable host of new followers of the

Saviour and Master we are privileged to serve. These are the true dimensions of our calling; and our most mundane activities must be seen against this sweeping backdrop.

The second thing promised to those who put true faith in Jesus is divine largesse, a rich response to petitions offered in Jesus' name, for the purpose of bringing glory to the Father (14:13–14). This theme reappears in several places, notably in 15:7–8,16 (cf. also 16:23–24); and I shall refrain from considering it until the fifth chapter of this book. It is important to observe even now, however, that this promise is for the one who puts his faith in Jesus as the revelation of God. Encouragement to believe is based on more than the need for faith if one is to enjoy new life, more than the importance of faith in overcoming troubled hearts. Encouragement to believe also makes its appeal by pointing to the splendid privileges that belong to believers: participation in the 'greater' works that flow from Christ's work, and participation in truly fruitful prayer. In short, knowledgeable, stable and triumphant faith is not merely some holding action which stabilizes troubled minds. Rather, it is the precondition for fruitful Christian life, for prayers with unction that call forth the blessing of the exalted Jesus.

All this comes about because Jesus culminates his work as the revelation of the Father by 'returning to the Father' via the cross. The work costs him dearly. Twice he reveals that he is himself deeply troubled in spirit (12:27; 13:21) as he contemplates the hours ahead; yet that same work constitutes the basis on which he can tell his disciples, 'Do not let *your* hearts be troubled. Trust in God; trust also in me' (14:1).

The Coming of the Spirit of Truth

'If you love me, you will obey what I command. I will ask the Father, and he will give you another Counsellor to be with you for ever – the Spirit of truth. The world cannot accept him, because it neither sees him nor knows him. But you know him, for he lives with you and will be in you. I will not leave you as orphans; I will come to you. Before long, the world will not see me any more, but you will see me. Because I live, you also will live. On that day you will realise that I am in my Father, and you are in me, and I am in you. Whoever has my commands and obeys them, he is the one who loves me. He who loves me will be loved by my Father, and I too will love him and show myself to him.'

Then Judas (not Judas Iscariot) said, 'But, Lord, why do you intend to show yourself to us and not to the world?'

Jesus replied, 'If anyone loves me, he will obey my teaching. My Father will love him, and we will come to him and make our home with him. He who does not love me will not obey my teaching. These words you hear are not my own; they belong to the Father who sent me.'

The first fourteen verses of John 14 find Jesus encouraging his disciples to exercise triumphant faith. Such faith apprehends who Jesus truly is, the revelation of the Father; and it trusts him, and thereby overcomes the troubled fear and malaise called forth by Jesus' references to his 'going away' to the Father. After all, Jesus will come back; and his 'departure' via the cross completes his mission and prepares a place in the Father's presence for the disciples. Jesus himself is thus the 'way' to the Father which they must take.

But his proffered comfort does not speak to the period that stretches out between Jesus' departure and his return; and it is to this gap that he now turns his attention. He promises to send in his place the Spirit of truth.

This is the first of several passages in the Farewell Discourse that discuss the Holy Spirit; and all of them refer to him as the *Paraclete* (14:15–21,25–27; 15:26–27; 16:7–15). The word *Paraclete* is a rough transliteration of the Greek *parakletos*, variously translated 'Comforter', 'Counsellor', 'Advocate', 'Helper'. I shall return to the significance of the title further on. For the moment it is sufficient to recognize that Jesus is concerned here with outlining to his disciples the arrangements he has made to help them during his absence, and that he is introducing a major theme which he will progressively develop.

Several emphases are intertwined in these verses. John presents Jesus as insisting on the following things:

The triune God makes himself present to the disciples of Jesus by the Spirit of truth

One of the most remarkable aspects of Jesus' teaching in this passage, however, is that it is the *triune God* who takes up his dwelling in the disciples of Jesus. This truth is unavoidable: 'I will ask the Father, and he will give you another Counsellor to be with you for ever – *the Spirit of truth*' (14:16–17a). So far we learn of the *Spirit's* involvement with the disciples, but no more. Two verses on, however, Jesus adds, '*I* will not leave you as orphans; *I* will come to you' (14:18). It is possible to suppose that Jesus is talking about his return at the resurrection (as appears to be the case in 14:19) or about his return at the end of the age (as in 14:3); but it is perhaps more likely that he is talking about being personally present with his disciples by means of the Spirit. After all, he promises not to abandon the disciples as orphans; and the section as a whole is concerned with the period between his departure and his ultimate return. More important and less ambiguous is verse 23: 'If anyone loves me, he will obey my teaching. *My Father* will love him, and we will come to him and make *our* home with him.' Here the Father and the Son take up their residence in the believer. All three Persons of the Godhead are thus involved.

The Old Testament writers were concerned that God should live with men. At the dedication of the temple, King Solomon, aware that God is utterly transcendent, cries out, 'But will God really dwell on earth? The heavens, even the highest heaven, cannot contain you. How much less this temple I have built!' (1 Kgs. 8:27). But although neither man nor his structures can contain God, nevertheless God may choose to live with men. The Old Testament prophets delight to look forward to the day when such intimacy will be commonplace. 'My dwelling-place will be with them; I will be their God, and they will be my people,' God promises; and Ezekiel faithfully records the promise (Ezek. 37:27). '"Shout and be glad, O Daughter of Zion. For I am coming, and I will live among you," declares the LORD' (Zech. 2:10). John insists that this occurred historically in the incarnation: 'The Word became flesh and lived for a while among us' (1:14). But now we are brought a stage further: this God reveals himself to the individual believer and takes up residence within him. 'I will ask the Father,' Jesus promises, 'and he will give you another Counsellor to be with you for ever – the Spirit of truth . . . If anyone loves me, he will obey my teaching. My Father will love him, and we will come to him and make our home with him' (14:16–17*a*, 23).

Other New Testament writers make much of the same glorious privilege. 'For we are the temple of the living God,' Paul writes. 'As God has said, "I will live with them and walk among them, and I will be their God, and they will be my people"'(2 Cor. 6:16; cf. Lev. 26:12; Jeremiah 32:38; Ezek. 37:27). Paul prays that the Father 'may strengthen you with power through his Spirit in your inner being, so that Christ may dwell in your hearts through faith' (Eph. 3:16–17*a*). Nor is such experience to be exclusively corporate. Even if an entire local church begins a slippery decline (Rev. 3:14–21), the exalted Christ still cries to the *individual* believer, 'Here I am! I stand at the door and knock. If *anyone* hears my voice and opens the door, I will go in and eat with him, and he with me' (Rev. 3:20).

This privilege is part of the blessing of the new age. It is part and parcel with the eternal life we already enjoy. That life awaits Christ's return for its consummation; and so also the privilege of experiencing God's dwelling with man awaits Christ's return for its consummation. Then we shall hear the stellar shout, 'Now the dwelling of God is with men, and he will live with them. They will be his people, and God himself will be with them and be their God. He will wipe every tear from their eyes. There will be no more death or mourning or crying or pain, for the old order of things has passed away' (Rev. 21:3–4).

Already, Jesus insists, that privilege is in some measure ours. A little later, just before his ascension, he again promises his followers, 'And surely I will be with you always, to the very end of the age' (Matt. 28:20). Christianity, it is true, is a religion based squarely in time-space history. It has a prepositional revelation, credal confessions, moral standards, missionary expeditions, corporate worship. But as essential as these are, one further feature must not be overlooked. Christianity claims that it is the means whereby a man may *know* God, and whereby God may come and make his home in a man. The thought of it is overwhelming; yet this is the heritage of every true believer.

Many religions promise some kind of mystical experience with deity. Often these religions claim that man is himself deified in some way in the process. The teaching of the fourth Gospel must be distinguished from such beliefs. John cannot envision knowing God, nor picture a man functioning as the dwelling of God, apart from the historical revelation of Jesus Christ, and the removal of sin by Jesus' return to the Father through the passion. Nevertheless, in our insistence on truth and on the central historical realities of our faith, we must not minimize the momentous promise of experiential fellowship with God. This intimacy, as we shall see, turns on our obedience (14:15,21,23); but it is no less real for that. We modern Christians badly need a deepening consciousness of God's sacred presence in us as much as we need moral renewal, historical awareness, and biblical and theological acuity.

> Love divine, all loves excelling,
> Joy of heaven, to earth come down,

Fix in us Thy humble dwelling,
All Thy faithful mercies crown.
Jesus, Thou art all compassion,
Pure, unbounded love Thou art;
Visit us with Thy salvation.
Enter every trembling heart.

Breathe, O breathe Thy loving Spirit
Into every troubled breast;
Let us all in Thee inherit,
Let us find the promised rest.
Take away the love of sinning;
Alpha and Omega be;
End of faith, as its Beginning,
Set our hearts at liberty.

Come, almighty to deliver,
Let us all Thy life receive;
Suddenly return, and never,
Never more Thy temples leave.
Thee we would be always blessing,
Serve Thee as Thy hosts above,
Pray, and praise Thee, without ceasing.
Glory in Thy perfect love.

Finish then Thy new creation:
Pure and spotless let us be;
Let us see Thy great salvation,
Perfectly restored in Thee.
Changed from glory into glory,
Till in heaven we take our place,
Till we cast our crowns before Thee,
Lost in wonder, love, and praise.

Charles Wesley (1707–88)

We are now very close to the sublime mystery of the Trinity, That the word *Trinity* is not found in the Scripture should occasion no alarm. The word itself is nothing more than a convenient way of referring to God as he has revealed himself: as one, unique, yet eternally existing in three persons all equally God, of one substance yet distinct in role.

Earlier in John's Gospel, we learn that all the persons of the Godhead are involved in Jesus' mission, albeit with distinct parts to play in the drama of redemption: 'For the one whom God has sent speaks the words of God; to him God gives the Spirit without limit. The Father loves the Son and has placed everything in his hands' (3:34–35). Here the Father loves the Son and sends the Son; the Son is loved and sent. The Father gives the Spirit to the Son, in measure unlimited. The Son receives him; and he speaks the words of God.

Where the focus is on the ministry of the Spirit, we again find all the persons of the Godhead involved (14:16–21,23–24). Jesus asks his Father to give the Spirit to the disciples; the Spirit is given, and is himself the means whereby the Father and the Son are present with and in the believers. Distinctions are simultaneously maintained and blurred: the Son is going away and therefore sends the Spirit as his replacement (distinction), yet the presence of the Spirit in the disciples is equally the presence of the Father and the Son (blur). Even if the word *Trinity* is not part of John's vocabulary, the ingredients of trinitarian faith are all there.

The Paraclete, the Spirit of truth, serves in many respects as the substitute for Jesus

This truth is made clear by three features. First, Jesus promises to send in his absence *'another* Paraclete'

(14:16). In English we have but one word for 'another'; in Greek there are two common words, and often they are distinguishable in meaning. For instance, in Galatians 1:6–7 Paul expresses astonishment that the Galatian believers could so quickly abandon the one who called them into the grace of Christ and turn to *'another* gospel: which is not *another'* (AV). The first 'another' really means a *different* gospel; and the second 'another' means 'a gospel *of the same kind'*. That is why the NIV renders the Galatians passage: 'turning to a different gospel – which is really no gospel at all.'

In John 14:16, the word for 'another' in the expression 'another Paraclete' is the same word as the second 'another' in Galatians 1:6–7. Jesus is promising not a *different* Paraclete but a Paraclete who is *essentially the same kind* that Jesus himself is.

This of course focuses our attention on the word *Paraclete*. In what sense is Jesus a Paraclete, and in what sense is the Holy Spirit another Paraclete of the same kind?

The word *Paraclete*, as I have indicated, is notoriously difficult to pin down. Etymologically the word seems to refer to 'one who is called alongside'; but etymology by itself rarely determines the meaning of a word. It is related to a verb which means 'to encourage' or 'to exhort'; so it is possible that a Paraclete is one who encourages or exhorts. The word is found in legal contexts: a Paraclete may be a legal adviser or counsellor, or perhaps on occasion a prosecuting attorney. This legal usage of the term predominates in extra-biblical literature.

The fact of the matter is that virtually all of these functions are explicitly ascribed to the Holy Spirit in the Farewell Discourse; and that is probably why the term *Paraclete* is used. The word boasts a wide range of meaning;

but it is rightly applied to the Holy Spirit, the Paraclete sent from the Father, because he is engaged in a wide range of activity on behalf of Jesus' disciples. We shall see that the Holy Spirit, as prosecuting attorney, exposes the sin of the world. He helps the believers in their witness, and strengthens and comforts them by his presence. He further explains the significance of Jesus' person and ministry, functioning as the agent of revelation. In all of these ministries the Holy Spirit is shown to be actively engaged (14:16–17,25–26; 15:26; 16:7–15).

To recognize these things prompts reflection on the second feature in these verses which shows us that the Paraclete serves in many respects as a substitute for Jesus. It is this: according to Jesus the promised Paraclete will do many of the things which Jesus himself does during his ministry. Will the Paraclete teach the disciples, guiding them into all truth (16:13)? But Jesus himself is known as the Teacher (e.g. 7:14; 13:13). Will the Paraclete bear witness to the truth before a watching world (15:26–27)? So also did Jesus during his ministry (e.g. 8:14). Will the Paraclete convict the world of its sin (16:8–11)? Jesus did the same (15:24). Moreover, even though it is the Paraclete who comes to be with the disciples for ever (14:16), this same Paraclete is the means by which Jesus himself, and his Father, make their home in the believer (14:23).

This is not to say that the functions of the Holy Spirit and the functions of the Son of God are precisely identical. Each of the two assumes some roles not assumed by the other. Only the Son became incarnate. Only he died and rose again. Only he intercedes for us before the Father's glory; for he himself suffered as the atoning sacrifice which turns away divine wrath, enabling deity both to be just and to justify the ungodly (Romans 3:21–25; 1 John 2:1–2). Indeed, the one New Testament passage which unambiguously calls Jesus a Paraclete (rendered 'one who speaks in our defence' in NIV) pictures Jesus in this role: 'But if anybody does sin, *we have one who speaks to the Father in our defence* – Jesus Christ, the Righteous One. He is the atoning sacrifice for our sins . . .' (1 John 2:1–2). The Holy Spirit intercedes for us in our weakness, interceding for the saints in accordance with God's will (Rom. 8:26); but this activity does not spring out of any atoning sacrifice which he himself has made, but out of his role as helper. Not all of Jesus' deeds can be repeated by the Holy Spirit.

On the other hand, during Jesus' ministry he was physically limited in space: if he was in Cana, he was not in Jericho or Caesarea. By contrast, the Holy Spirit in discharging his ministry to us is not limited by space: he simultaneously indwells believers in Montreal and Moscow, Baltimore and Burton-on-Trent. Some of the Spirit's ministry could not have been duplicated by Jesus during his ministry on earth.

Nevertheless, when all the qualifications have been made, a careful reading of John's Gospel shows us that the Paraclete whom Jesus promises does many things for the disciples that Jesus himself did; and in so doing he serves as a substitute for Jesus.

The third feature lies in the title given to this Paraclete: he is the Spirit of truth (14:17). The expression is used three times in the fourth Gospel, always with reference to the Paraclete (14:17; 15:26; 16:13). The expression is a pregnant one, especially since Jesus has just claimed to be the truth (14:6). Yet the expression 'Spirit of truth' certainly means more than 'Spirit of Jesus, who is the truth'. This becomes clear when we examine the contexts of the two other passages where the title occurs. 'When the Counsellor [Paraclete] comes . . . the Spirit of truth who goes out from the Father, *he will testify about me'* (15:26). 'I have much more to say to you, more than you can now bear. But when he, the Spirit of truth, comes, *He will guide you into all truth.* He will not speak on his own; he will speak only what he hears, and *he will tell you* what is yet to come' (16:12–13). In other words, the Spirit of truth is the Spirit who communicates truth. In particular he communicates further truth concerning the significance of Jesus' mission – truth the disciples are not yet able to bear.

We ought to delight in the fact that Jesus designated this other Paraclete as the Spirit *of truth*. If the Holy Spirit is the one who completes the revelation of Jesus Christ by explaining things the disciples could not then bear to hear (16:12–15), then it is reassuring to learn that truth characterizes him; for we may be sure his testimony will be true. Just as Jesus authenticates the veracity of the biblical revelation before him (e.g. Matthew 5:17–20; John 10:35), so also he authenticates the veracity of the biblical revelation still to come.

The Paraclete, the Spirit of truth, is thus an admirable substitute for Jesus. He ministers to the disciples in many of the ways Jesus did; but in particular he communicates to them the fullest explanation of Jesus' mission. Even the mysteries surrounding Jesus' 'departure' will become clear once the Spirit of truth has elucidated the matter. In these many ways the promised Paraclete is the appropriate substitute for Jesus.

Perhaps one of the most wonderful aspects of Jesus' promise to ask the Father to send another Counsellor (Paraclete) is that Jesus should bother to make the promise at all. He could have simply sent the Holy Spirit without first being so solicitous of his disciples' confusion and grief. After all, it is Jesus who faces Gethsemane and the cross, not they. Yet here he consoles them: 'I will not leave you as orphans' (14:18) – without provision, without love, without a guardian and helper, without a protector and counsellor, without an explanation of these momentous events unfolding before their eyes. He promises, 'I will come to you' (14:18) – not only at the end of the age, but in the person of the Paraclete, the Holy Spirit sent as successor of Jesus, and in many respects substitute for Jesus.

We cannot help but ask ourselves at this point if we worship God the Holy Spirit and accord him the reverence and love we offer the Father and the Son. The successor Jesus has appointed is not ill-suited to his task. Far from it: he is to be to us what Jesus was to his own disciples during the days of his flesh. Let us worship, and be thankful.

The Spirit of truth, who cannot be seen, for ever lives in and with the disciples of Jesus

The purpose of Jesus' request to his Father, that the Father might send the Spirit, is that this Counsellor might be with the disciples of Jesus for ever (14:16). No transient gift, this: the blessed Paraclete comes to us not just in our best moments, nor exclusively in times of crushing need, but always and for ever. The Holy Spirit is given in order that the divine presence may be with the disciples for ever. 'You know him,' Jesus then assures his followers, 'for he lives with you and will be in you' (14:17).

There are variant readings in the text for these last two verbs. The words 'for he *lives* with you' could be 'for he *will live* with you' (all that is required in Greek for the change of tense is a change of accent); and the words 'and *will be* in you' are displaced in many manuscripts by 'and *is* in you'. I suspect the scholarly debate in this case makes little difference to the meaning. John's Gospel clearly insists that the Holy Spirit was not given until Jesus was glorified (7:39); so it is unlikely that John is here arguing that the disciples enjoyed the Holy Spirit's presence *before* Jesus' glorification. Within this passage itself Jesus promises that he will ask the Father to send another Counsellor: the presupposition is that, when Jesus is speaking, this other Counsellor has not yet come.

The truth of the matter is that John regularly puts things in the present tense even when he is referring to the future. The cross, the resurrection, the ascension and glorification, the subsequent sending of the Holy Spirit – all of these are seen as one grand event. Indeed, this event looms so large in the thinking of Jesus that in the period leading up to it he begins to speak of it as already having taken place, or at least as if it were in the process of taking place. A few days earlier, still quite some time before the passion, Jesus can look forward towards it with a strange mixture of tenses: '*Now* my heart *is* troubled, and what shall I say? "Father, save me from *this hour*"? No, it was for this very reason I came to *this hour*. . . . *Now is* the time for judgment on this world; *now* the prince of this world *will be driven out*. But I, *when* I am lifted up from the earth, *will draw* all men to myself (12:27,31–32).

In English we sometimes use the present tense to refer to the future. 'I'm going into the city tomorrow', we say, instead of 'I will go into the city tomorrow'. In a similar way, it is not unlikely that the verbs in verse 17 are present tense, but with a future meaning: the Holy Spirit will live with you and will be in you. Perhaps some later scribe, perceiving that this was the meaning, tampered with his manuscripts to make the text explicitly future: that could account for the textual variants.

What is more important is that Jesus can speak of the Holy Spirit being *with* the disciples and *in* the disciples. This distinction is important. It is not that 'with you' refers to the presence of the Holy Spirit in the church, whereas 'in you' refers to the presence of the Holy Spirit in the individual Christian; for 'with you' and 'in you' could apply equally both to the church and to the believer. 'With you' suggests rather an association, a personal sharing, some kind of fellowship; 'in you' suggests real indwelling. Christians enjoy intimate association with the Holy Spirit; and simultaneously they constitute a dwelling for him.

It is important to retain both perspectives. Where the first is lost, and we speak only of the Spirit 'in' us, there is a tendency to slide towards a mysticism which does not adequately distinguish between the Holy Spirit and ourselves. Our desires, our hopes, our wills may then be indistinguishable in our minds from the desires and promptings of the Holy Spirit. In the worst case a man deifies himself; which results in either the birth of a new religion, like Eckankar with its roots in Hinduism, or else a megalomaniacal madness of the kind which produced Jim Jones.

Where the first is retained at the expense of the second, and people speak only of the Spirit 'with' them but not 'in' them, the marvel of the Spirit's condescension and operation in the New Testament are easily overlooked. Jesus did not ask his Father to send a Paraclete who would only be *with* them. His disciples need more than that: they need the very presence within them of the one who gives them new life, sanctifies them. This Paraclete makes the presence of deity so immediate (the triune God indwelling man by the Spirit!) that they need never again see themselves as abandoned orphans.

The Holy Spirit, then, is both external to us and yet within us. That he is external to us preserves his transcendence, preserves the ontological gap between God and ourselves. Though he chooses to live within us, he cannot be reduced to such narrow confines; and if he could, either we would be God or he would not be God. Moreover, the fact that he is external to us, yet within us, sets the stage for some of his other roles. For example, when he convicts the world of sin (16:8) he may do this through our witness – but he may do it independently of our witness.

That he chooses to live within us lies at the centre of Christian experience and hope. We have already seen in this chapter that the triune God makes himself present to the disciples of Jesus by means of the Holy Spirit. The Holy Spirit is thus the one by whom we already taste something of the bliss of the age to come, when our knowledge of God will be unimpeded. The essence of eternal life is truly to know God, and Jesus Christ whom God sent (17:3); and now in the period between the passion/glorification of Jesus and his return, we enjoy an anticipatory taste of this knowledge by means of the Spirit. That is why Paul can repeatedly refer to the Holy Spirit as the 'down payment' of our promised inheritance (e.g. 2 Cor. 1:22; 5:5; Eph. 1:14): he is merely elucidating what Jesus himself taught.

Perhaps this is what is meant by the final words of verse 19: 'Because I live, you also will live.' The verse is admittedly ambiguous, but it may best be taken in this sense: 'Before long, the world will not see me any more (i.e., after my death the "world" will not see me, since in my resurrection form I will not show myself to the world; and then I will ascend to my Father, where the world can certainly not see me at all), but you will see me (i.e., after my resurrection, you believers will see me).[2] Because I live (i.e., after my resurrection), you also will live (i.e., because of my resurrection, to which you shall be witnesses, I shall ascend and ask the Father to send the Paraclete, who will give you life as well – life to be enjoyed now, even if it is to be consummated only at my return).' As Jesus says later, 'It is for your good that I am going away. Unless I go away, the Counsellor will not come to you; but if I go, I will send him to you' (16:7).

The Holy Spirit has many functions. More of them are unpacked and laid out in later sections of the Farewell Discourse, and still others are scattered throughout the New Testament. But most of them are related to this first rich promise: the Holy Spirit is given as the one who lives with the disciples of Jesus, and in them.

The world and the disciples of Jesus relate differently to the Spirit of truth

'The world cannot accept him, because it neither sees him nor knows him. But you know him, for he lives with you and will be in you. . . . Whoever has my commands and obeys them, he is the one who loves me. He who loves me will be loved by my Father, and I too will love him and show myself to him' (14:17, 21).

This prompts a question from Judas (not Judas Iscariot, who has already left the room, 13:30), who is mentioned elsewhere in Luke 6:16 and Acts 1:13: 'But, Lord, why do you intend to show yourself to us and not to the world?' (14:22). The question in Judas's mind is probably general, without any attempt to distinguish between Jesus' manifestation in resurrection form and his manifestation by the Spirit. The problem Judas faces is that he cannot imagine how the Messiah, popularly conceived, could show himself to devotees but not to the world; nor why he should want to. If Jesus is the

Messiah, will he not throw off the might of Rome and lead the people and nation into glorious ascendancy surpassing even the zenith of the reigns of David and Solomon? How could the Messiah have a retiring nature? In the same vein, had not Jesus' own brothers earlier protested, 'No-one who wants to become a public figure acts in secret. Since you are doing these things, show yourself to the world' (7:4)? The real question in the mind of Judas, therefore, concerns the nature and validity of Jesus' Messiahship, not the distinction between his coming to his disciples after the resurrection and his coming to the disciples by the Spirit.

The reply is presented in terms of the latter, but with emphasis on the contrast between unbelievers and the disciples: 'If anyone loves me, he will obey my teaching. My Father will love him, and we will come to him and make our home with him. He who does not love me will not obey my teaching' (14:23–24*a*). Judas calls in question the validity of Jesus' Messiahship; Jesus implicitly calls in question the validity of his followers' discipleship.

It is extremely important to understand what John means by the word 'world'. Except for a few instances where the 'world' refers to the physical earth, the created globe, the word always has a negative value. The 'world' in John is a symbol for all that is in rebellion against God, all that is loveless and disobedient, all that is selfish and sinful. When we read therefore in John 3:16 that 'God so loved the *world* that he gave his one and only Son', we are not to think that God's love is being praised by reference to the world's bigness, but by reference to its badness. This ugly, sinful, rebellious world, this sewer of infidelity, this glut of endless selfishness, this habitation of cruelty, this lover of violence, this promoter of greed, this maker of idols – this world God loved, and loved so much that he sent his Son.

This world, Jesus says, cannot accept the Spirit of truth, because it neither sees him nor knows him (14:17). Who, then, can receive the Spirit? The answer is repeated again and again. *'If you love me, you will obey* what I command. I will ask the Father, and he will give you another Counsellor to be with you for ever' (14:15–16). 'Whoever *has my commands and obeys them*, he is the one who *loves me. He who loves me* will be loved by my Father, and I too will love him and show myself to him' (14:21). *'If anyone loves me, he will obey my teaching.* My Father will love him, and we will come to him and make our home with him. He who does not love me will not obey my teaching' (14:23–24*a*).

In other words, the one who loves Jesus obeys his teaching; and it is to this person alone that Jesus manifests himself by the Holy Spirit. The one who does not love Jesus does not obey his teaching; and such a person is identified with the world and cannot accept the Spirit of truth. The world stands for mankind over against God; and the Spirit of truth is so alien to this wretched world that the world cannot recognize him. The tragedy lies in the circularity of the dilemma: because a person does not love Christ, he is closed to Christ's teaching; that teaching concerns, in part, the Spirit by whom Christ manifests himself. As a result such a person, ignorant of the Spirit, is not aware of Christ and his teaching. The person who belongs to the world is claimed by this wretched circle, a circle spawned by his own unbelief, disobedience and self-love. The thought is very close to the seemingly hopeless condition described by Paul: 'The man without the Spirit does not accept the things that come from the Spirit of God, for they are foolishness to him and he cannot understand them, because they are spiritually discerned' (1 Cor. 2:14).

Two very important observations spring from this contrast between the believer and the world. The first is explicitly made in the text. It is this: the believer's growth in the knowledge of God and in the experience of the Holy Spirit turns at least in part on his love for Christ and obedience to him. Deep knowledge of divine tidings cannot be acquired by *mere* study and careful observation.

Some modern Evangelicals give the impression that the only essential factor in winning men to Christ is the proclamation of the gospel in appropriate garb. They seem to think that if only the church learns to witness appropriately to the various peoples of the world, vast numbers of men and women will certainly be saved. I applaud their efforts to make us aware of the profound cultural barriers that render articulation of the gospel far more difficult than is sometimes thought. Their isolation and identification of such barriers will help the Christian witness to avoid needless negative reactions, and help ensure that when he causes offence it is the truth of the gospel which has evoked it, not his own maladroit offensiveness. But when all caveats are in, it is sobering to remember that the apostle John is not so sanguine about the receptivity of the world. The fourth Gospel does not encourage us in the notion that proper communication is necessarily effective communication.

Knowledge of chemistry, physics, or English literature depends on the acquisition of facts, and on the accumulation of experience in weighing those facts. Knowledge of holy things, on the other hand, depends no less on love for Christ and on obedience to him. Jesus insists that the world hates him because he testifies that its deeds are evil (7:7) – not because of overwhelming epistemological objections. At one point, Jesus charges, '*Because* I tell the truth, you do not believe me!' (8:45). No more sorry indictment is possible. It would be sad enough if, *despite* the fact that Jesus tells the truth, he is not believed; but if, *because* he tells the truth, he is not believed, then the mere enunciation of the truth by the most gifted communicators cannot ensure any result other than multiplying hatred directed towards him. The world cannot accept the Spirit of truth.

By contrast, the true disciples of Jesus love him; and the entailment of that love is obedience to him. As a function of this loving obedience, such disciples are granted the Spirit of truth, the Counsellor, who will live with them and be in them. The one who loves Jesus is loved by the Father; and the Triune God takes up his dwelling in him (14:21,23). It has always been so, for God declares, 'I love those who love me, and those who seek me find me' (Prov. 8:17).

If God's best blessings are designed for those who love his Son and are obedient to him, it becomes clear that verse 15 has not been placed where it is by sheer accident or rambling thoughtlessness. The verse follows the great promises that those who have faith in Christ will do greater tidings than Christ himself does, and will learn to pray effectively in Jesus' name. The same verse precedes Jesus' promise to ask the Father to send another Counsellor, the Spirit of truth. In other words, the injunction to love and obey Christ is surrounded by promises; or, otherwise conceived, at the heart of the promises is the presupposition that the recipients of the promises will love Jesus and obey him. It appears, too, as if loving Jesus, obeying Jesus and having faith in Jesus constitute elements of an indivisible whole. It is impossible truly to love him without trusting him and obeying him. It is impossible truly to obey him without loving him and trusting him. It is impossible truly to trust him without loving and obeying him. But the one who truly loves, obeys and trusts Jesus Christ is the one who receives the Spirit of truth and the blessings he brings.

The second observation that springs from the contrast between the believer and the world in this passage is implicit, but important: the passage does not concern itself with explaining how a member of the world becomes a disciple of Jesus Christ.

Up to this point one might almost think that the world and the believers constitute two groups so mutually exclusive that a person could never pass from one to the other. The people of the world are blind to the Spirit's appearance, and deaf to his voice: how can they ever break the chains of the world? At this juncture it is essential to remember that every true disciple once belonged to the world; so it must be possible to escape the world's corruptions. Every believer is a testimony to that fact. As Jesus himself put it a little later, 'You do not belong to the world, but I have chosen you out of the world' (15:19).

Yet when we read the words, 'Whoever has my commands and obeys them, he is the one who loves me. He who loves me will be loved by my Father, and I too will love him and show myself to him' (14:21), we must not think that we may somehow win the Father's love and Jesus' love by being obedient and loving. We cannot wrest God's love from him by our obedience; and if we could, it would not be worth having. The truth of the matter is that God loved *the world* so much he sent his Son (3:16): while we were still sinners, Christ died for us. John comments elsewhere, 'This is love: not that we loved God, but that he loved us and sent his Son as an atoning sacrifice for our sins' (1 John 4:10). But once a person has become a follower of Jesus, he must understand that such a relationship is characterized by faith, love and obedience, and that within this framework he experiences God's love in a special way. The unbelieving world, by contrast, can look forward only to God's wrath (3:36).

But John 14:15–24 does not discuss how a person escapes the world and becomes a follower of Jesus. That discussion is pursued further on, where we learn, among other things, that the disciple of Jesus is chosen out of the world (15:19), and is the object of the Christian's witness (15:26–27) and the Counsellor's convicting ministry (16:8–11). The passage at hand does not concern itself with such matters. It is interested only in the contrast between the two communities, the community of the world and the community of Christ. This contrast is of utmost importance. There are two communities, and only two. The passage therefore forces Christians to examine themselves to see if their life is characterized by love for Christ, obedience to Christ, and faith in Christ, and by a deepening awareness of the fathomless depths of God's love; or by worldliness as the fourth Gospel presents it. There is no middle ground, however strenuously we may seek to carve one out. The stark duality confronts us with an unsparing demand for wholehearted commitment. If it declines to comment on such anomalies as the temporary backslider or the believer who remains on a liquid diet long after he should have graduated to solid foods (e.g. Heb. 5:11–14), at least it portrays unambiguously that one is either a child of God or a child of the devil, a follower of Jesus or a follower of the world, a person who enjoys the presence of the Spirit of truth or a person who cannot accept him. All the rest is qualified explanation or lame excuse.

The world and the disciples of Jesus relate differently to the Spirit of truth.

The Spirit of truth is granted by the Father to the believers because of Jesus' death/resurrection/exaltation and intercession

'I will ask the Father, and he will give you another Counsellor to be with you for ever – the Spirit of truth' (14:16–17). Such 'asking' is of course conditioned by Jesus' departure, his 'going away'; for he later says, 'It is for your good that I am going away. Unless I go away, the Counsellor will not come to you; but if I go, I will send him to you' (16:7). As John explains, the Holy Spirit could come only after Jesus was glorified (7:39). Once Jesus' 'going away', his death/resurrection/exaltation, has occurred, he will send the Counsellor (16:7), or ask the Father to send him (14:16). In other words, both the Father and the Son are involved in sending the Holy Spirit (cf. 15:26); but this event takes place only as a result of Christ's cross-work and triumph.

The theme of redemption is rather subtly blended into the fabric of John's Gospel. We observed some of its features in the last chapter; now it has returned in a new guise. Jesus once taught, 'The hour has come for the Son of Man to be glorified. I tell you the truth, unless an ear of wheat falls to the ground and dies, it remains only a single seed. But if it dies, it produces many seeds' (12:23–24). Jesus is now about to be 'glorified' by way of the cross; and in this death/resurrection/exaltation, Jesus' new life spells life for the believers: 'Because I live,' Jesus insists, 'you also will live' (14:19). The means by which the victorious gains of Jesus' glorification are bestowed on his followers is the commissioning of the Holy Spirit.

But this presupposes that the Holy Spirit could not possibly have been sent had it not been for Christ's cross-work, resurrection and exaltation. The successful completion of Christ's mission makes the Spirit's mission possible. This, too, tells convincingly against any interpretation of these verses which makes the Spirit's coming to the believer in any way dependent on the believer's meritorious conduct. Rather, the Spirit descends on believers because of Christ's death/resurrection/exaltation, his triumphant return to the Father's presence, redemption accomplished; and those on whom he descends, far from being the cause of his coming, are characterized by a certain relationship to Jesus, a relationship of love, obedience and trust. Those who profess to be believers must take it as their responsibility to love Jesus, obey him and trust him; but they must not think that by so doing they earn his favour and his gifts. These spring from his own triumphant 'going away' via the cross, and from the intercession that the Father on that basis could not possibly deny.

We have returned to the mystery of the Trinity. God is one; yet he has revealed himself to be of one substance, but eternally existing in three Persons. What these verses – and indeed much of the fourth Gospel – show is that at each point in the plan of redemption, all three Persons of the Godhead have been at work on our behalf. The Father loves the Son; but he also loves the world, even though that world is characterized by rebellion and wickedness. He loves this world so much that he sends his Son as its Redeemer, and he loves his Son and gives all things into his hands. The Spirit comes upon the Son in an exhaustive manner, enabling the incarnate Son to fulfil his mission, and serving as public testimony that Jesus is indeed the anointed Son of God. The Son dies, a willing sacrifice, the atonement for sin; and thus he demonstrates the immensity of his own love for us: 'Having loved his own who were in the world, he now showed them the full extent of his love' (13:1).

Returning by the resurrection and ascension to the Father's presence, to the glory he enjoyed with his Father before the resurrection, he intercedes with his Father on our behalf, and along with his Father sends the Holy Spirit as another Counsellor. Even in this gift, the Son has not abandoned us as orphans: the gift of the Holy Spirit is a mark of the love of the Son and of the Father, even as it is the result of the Son's triumph on the cross. And this Holy Spirit, this Counsellor, comes to us as the one who now makes the presence of the Son and of the Father real to us.

Our finite minds, even extended to their fullest powers, barely comprehend the separate statements. To appreciate fully the breadth and depth and wholeness of salvation's plan, to worship adequately the triune God who effects it, will be the work of eternity: indeed, eternity itself will be too short.

> We give immortal praise
>   To God the Father's love,
> For all our comforts here,
>   And better hopes above.
> He sent his own eternal Son
> To die for sins that we had done.
>
> To God the Son belongs
>   Immortal glory too,
> Who bought us with his blood
>   From everlasting woe;
> And now he lives, and now he reigns,
> And sees the fruit of all his pains.
>
> To God the Spirit's name
>   Immortal worship give,
> Whose new-creating power

Makes the dead sinner live.
His work completes the grand design
And fills the soul with joy divine.

Almighty God, to Thee
  Be endless honours done,
The undivided Three
  And the mysterious One.
Where reason fails, with all her powers,
There faith prevails and love adores.

Isaac Watts (1674–1748)

The revelation of these truths is itself a reflection of the revelation of God through Jesus Christ

The section ends with the sentence, 'These words you hear are not my own; they belong to the Father who sent me' (14:24*b*). The Greek text actually speaks of the *word* or *message* you hear, rather than the *words* (plural). Jesus is assuring his disciples that even this 'word' from him is not the product of a versatile imagination, but the message which the Father gave him to give to us. It is nothing less than God's Word.

The verse calls to mind earlier emphases in John 14, explored in the second chapter of this book. Jesus is the revelation of the Father, the one who in his very being expounds the Father to men; but precisely because he is so dependent on his Father, everything he speaks and does is no less and no more than the Father's speaking and doing. Jesus assures his disciples that his teaching on the coming Counsellor belongs to the same category as his other teaching: its ultimate origin is the Father. The Son is not acting independently in executing the plan of redemption, rather he is working in profound harmony with his Father, and so all he teaches is precisely the Word of God. Certainty is thereby made doubly sure; quivering faith is granted a greater rock on which to rest. And unbelief is made the more heinous.

Note: In the exposition of this passage I have assumed that the Holy Spirit is a person, and that traditional trinitarian formulations are both biblical and true. I have not attempted to defend the doctrine of the Trinity (except perhaps implicitly), nor have I attempted to prove that the Holy Spirit is a person. This is because the passage before us does not have such matters as their chief concerns, even though, in my view, it presupposes their essential ingredients.

It may be helpful to list a few reasons why I believe the Scriptures teach the Holy Spirit is both a person and divine. This list is neither exhaustive nor detailed; but it reflects several quite different lines of reasoning which, combined, are convincing.

First, both in this passage and in many others, the Holy Spirit performs personal actions. The Paraclete is a person who comes as Jesus' successor and, in many respects, substitute: a mere influence, or anything less personal and less divine than Jesus Christ himself, would necessarily be something of a disappointment.

Second, the Holy Spirit enjoys both the distinctness from the Father and the oneness with the Father that the Son enjoys. The distinctness (e.g. the Father sends the Spirit in response to the Son's intercession) ensures his separate personality; his oneness (e.g. by the Spirit's indwelling in the believer, the Father and the Son also make their home in the believer) ensures his deity.

Third, according to Matthew 12:31–32, a person may sin against the Holy Spirit. Contextually this is more than sinning against the light, or the like. It suggests again (though it does not prove) that the Holy Spirit is a person.

Fourth, the trinitarian formulae in the New Testament are virtually inexplicable if the Holy Spirit, like the Father and Son, is not both a person and divine. I refer to such expressions as 'baptizing them in the name of the Father and of the Son and of the Holy Spirit' (Matt. 28:19) and 'May the grace of the Lord Jesus Christ, and the love of God, and the fellowship of the Holy Spirit be with you all' (2 Cor. 13:14). To construe the Spirit as less than person and less than divine when the texts put him in the company of deity and speak of his name would be as foolish as to say, 'I baptize you in the name of the Father, and of the Son, and of lovely influences.' The thought approaches blasphemy.

Fifth, although the Holy Spirit is sent from the Father, such 'sentness' does not reduce the Counsellor to the status of a thing. After all, John's Gospel makes much of the fact that Jesus himself was sent (e.g. 3:17); and the Gospels do not think of Jesus as impersonal. More to the point, the New Testament writers regularly distinguish between the Holy Spirit and his gifts (e.g. 1 Cor. 12:7–11). Concerning these gifts, Paul writes, 'All these are the work of one and the same Spirit, and he gives them to each man, just as he determines' (1 Cor. 12:11).

Sixth, older theologians sometimes point to embodiments of the Holy Spirit. At Jesus' baptism, for instance, 'the Holy Spirit descended on him in bodily form like a dove' (Luke 3:22). It is possible, I suppose, to think of

God sending a dove to represent a divine blessing or influence or the like; but the language suggests something more: the Holy Spirit descended in bodily form like a dove. It is difficult to predicate such a thing of an influence. The most natural way to take the passage is to think of the Holy Spirit as a person who normally has no bodily form.

Seventh, there are many isolated passages which do not easily fit into one of the previous categories, but which make the best sense if we presuppose both that the Holy Spirit is a person and that the Holy Spirit is God. One example must suffice. In Acts 5:3–4, Peter asks Ananias, 'Ananias, how is it that Satan has so filled your heart that you have *lied to the Holy Spirit* . . .? You have not lied to men *but to God*.' The parallel is obvious.

Three Clarifications

'All this I have spoken while still with you. But the Counsellor, the Holy Spirit, whom the Father will send in my name, will teach you all things and will remind you of everything I have said to you. Peace I leave with you; my peace I give you. I do not give to you as the world gives. Do not let your hearts be troubled and do not be afraid.

'You heard me say, "I am going away and I am coming back to you." If you loved me, you would be glad that I am going to the Father, for the Father is greater than I. I have told you now before it happens, so that when it does happen you will believe. I will not speak with you much longer, for the prince of this world is coming. He has no hold on me, but the world must learn that I love the Father and that I do exactly what my Father has commanded me. Come now; let us leave.'

Good. teacher that he is, Jesus knows when to press on with new material, and when to pause for review, clarification and expansion. Something of the latter is reflected in these verses (14:25–31). Up to now, Jesus has been trying to quell the fears, anxieties and confusion of his disciples. His departure, he explains, is temporary, and for their good. The 'going away' itself accomplishes the climactic step of his mission and prepares a place in the presence of God for his followers. Understanding these things, he has said, presupposes that they understand who Jesus really is; and, perceiving their incomprehension, Jesus repeats and briefly explains his claims. As for the period when he will be away, he promises to send another Counsellor, the Holy Spirit, to stand in for him; and that Counsellor will be the means by which the Triune God will make his purpose known to Jesus' followers.

Not surprisingly, Jesus' words so far have revealed little of what life will be like for the disciples until Jesus returns. They are clearly expected to continue in love and obedience towards Jesus, and to exercise faith in him (14:12,15,23); they will learn to pray (14:13–14) and enjoy the presence of the Spirit (14:17,23). But much more needs to be said. They need to have their horizons expanded. They must glimpse that because of Jesus' 'going away', because of his atoning death and his triumphant resurrection and exaltation, his disciples are poised to embark on a world-wide mission empowered by the Spirit. To this panoramic vision Jesus must shortly turn. He will then explain something of the intimacy his disciples will continue to enjoy with him, an intimacy which, like that between a vine and its branches, issues in tremendous fruitfulness (15:1–16).

Not everything, Jesus will explain, is sweetness and light: his disciples in their continuing witness to the world must expect the world's opposition. Fruit there will be; but there will also be hatred, persecution, even torture and death. But such bleak prospects become bearable in so far as they constitute evidence that Jesus' disciples naturally belong to a different sphere, and boast a heavenly allegiance, confessing a lordship that stands in opposition to the world (15:17 – 16:4). Even here the Counsellor will continue with Christ's people. He will work in the world and drive home conviction of sin, something Jesus was able to do so superbly; and the Spirit will complete the revelation of the triune God in its supreme manifestation in Jesus Christ, so that the disciples will not lack the necessary understanding of these central redemptive events (16:5–15). And then once more Jesus will focus attention on the immediate future: he will point to the cross (16:16–33).

Sometimes in our darkest hours what we most need to see is the panorama of redemptive history, the unfolding of events according to God's gracious plan to call out a people for himself. Our narrow introspection funnels our vision into myopic self-concern; the breath-taking vista of God's perspective on human history makes us perceive things we could not have imagined, and captures our thoughts and affections with the holy power of truth. We begin to feel a part of the whole – a small part, perhaps, but at least a significant part. Then the bitter frustration of temporary defeat dissipates as events take on their true proportion, and we escape the paralysing claustrophobia of self-love. Preachers, teachers and other believers who help us see God's reality with such clear vision serve us well. Jesus exercises this sort of ministry to his own disciples in chapters 15 and 16.

But before turning his attention in this direction, Jesus again takes up the themes he has already introduced. This is not to say this passage is redundant. Quite the contrary: Jesus takes the subjects he has treated so far and develops them by adding more content and clarifying points the disciples have obviously missed.

Three points are stressed:

Jesus departs, but he leaves his followers large bequests

'All this I have spoken while still with you' (14:25), Jesus says; and no doubt the 'all this' refers to what he has said so far. But this opening sentence also jolts the disciples back to the question of Jesus' departure. Jesus has been talking about some kind of continued intimate relationship with his disciples; he now pauses to warn them that, although he may say all of these things, he is not cancelling his departure plans. But if the disciples cannot grasp all he is saying, at least they may be assured that the things of which he speaks will be further explicated with the coming of the Counsellor, the Holy Spirit (14:26).

By this means the first of the two 'large bequests' specifically mentioned is introduced.

1. The Holy Spirit. 'But the Counsellor, the Holy Spirit, whom the Father will send in my name, will teach you all things and will remind you of everything I have said to you' (14:26).

This is the second mention of the Paraclete (Counsellor): cf. 14:16–18. In the earlier passage we learnt, among other things, that Jesus would ask the Father, and the Father would send 'another Counsellor' (14:16). The same thing is now expressed in a slightly different way: the Father will send the Counsellor, Jesus says, 'in my name' (14:26). In its context, the phrase 'in my name' cannot refer to the disciples' requests to the Counsellor, uttered 'in my name'. It is true that believers are to pray 'in my name' (14:13); but that is not in view here. Either 'in my name' in 14:26 suggests the Father sends the Spirit as a result of Jesus' prayer (in which case 14:26 is repeating the content of 14:16), or else 'in my name' does not explain *why* the Father sent the Spirit, but *the purpose for which he sent the Spirit*. In that case 'in my name' means something like 'with my authority, to act in my place', or the like. That is very close to the meaning of the phrase in Mark 13:6: 'Many will come *in my name,* claiming, "I am he," and will deceive many.' These deceivers come purporting to act *in Jesus' place*, claiming to act *with his authority*. Their claims are false; but the Spirit who comes in Jesus' name really does act in Jesus' place and with his authority.

In any case, there are two new things introduced concerning this Counsellor.

a. His description. He is referred to for the first time in John's Gospel as the *Holy* Spirit. In fact, in this Gospel the Counsellor is so designated only here and in 20:22. The adjective *holy* as applied to the Spirit is partly titular; but it designates that the Spirit in question is the Spirit of God, and simultaneously reflects this Spirit's character. He is the *Holy* Spirit, not just the Spirit of truth or the Spirit of power.

The Father is *holy* (17:11) and righteous (17:25), and is so addressed by the Son. Jesus is the *Holy* One of God (Mark 1:24; Luke 4:34); and the Counsellor is the *Holy* Spirit. The highest orders of angels constantly pour out their praise before the throne of the Deity and never stop crying, day and night, 'Holy, Holy, Holy!' (Rev. 4:8). It is both wonderful and frightening to hear the voice of God intoning. 'Be holy because I, the LORD your God, am holy' (Lev. 19:2).

It has long been recognized that the word *holy* brings with it the fragrance of transcendence. If a man is holy, he is more than moral: he belongs to God. If the tabernacle in the wilderness has a most holy place within its curtained walls, that place is not simply cleaner or purer, but the place where the transcendent God chooses to manifest himself in a particularly intense and focused way. Derivatively, the word *holy* refers to purity of life, thought and conduct; but it never loses its more fundamental significance. Therefore the purity in view is based on God himself, on belonging to God or relating to him in some way.

The passage before us does not make much of the title given to the Counsellor, the Holy Spirit. From within a broader, biblical framework, however, Christians ought to rejoice in the rubric. The Counsellor sent by the Father in Jesus' name is holy: and in his case the ascription is as absolute as it is in the case of the Father or the Son. He is holy because he is God. Small wonder he brings conviction to the sinful world (16:8–11); small wonder his presence in our lives not only ensures our progressive growth in holy ways, but brings on absolute demand: 'Do you not know that your body is a temple of the *Holy* Spirit, who is in you, whom you have received from God?' (1 Cor. 6:19).

b. His function. The Counsellor, Jesus promises his disciples, 'will teach you all things and will remind you of everything I have said to you' (14:26). We have already been exposed to this thought in considering the implications of the title, 'the Spirit of truth' (14:17); but now this fundamental function of the Holy Spirit is explicitly spelt out. Here, we read, he *teaches* all things; later, we learn, he *guides* into all truth (16:13), *speaks* what he hears (16:13) and *makes known* or *announces* what is Christ's (16:13–14). The thought is the same: one primary function of the Counsellor is to teach. Even in the Old Testament God gave his good Spirit to instruct the people (Neh. 9:20); but here the thought is bound up with the revelation of Christ.

This begins to be clear when we ask what 'all things' means: the Holy Spirit will teach the disciples 'all things'. This cannot mean all things without exception. The Holy Spirit is not particularly concerned to impart to the disciples of Jesus an exhaustive knowledge of nuclear physics, astronomy, cell biology, the literature of Tanzania, or the mating habits of the porcupine. Moreover, even if he had the inclination to attempt this transfer of knowledge, we would not be able to receive it; for our finiteness precludes the attribute of omniscience.

The Holy Spirit teaches Jesus' disciples all things – all things, that is to say, that they need to know about the troubling events taking place, all things concerning the revelation of Jesus Christ that are still at this point subject to so much misunderstanding, all things that will quiet their fears by informing their minds. In particular, Jesus promises, the Holy Spirit will remind the disciples of everything Jesus himself taught them.

There are four important implications of this and similar statements in the Farewell Discourse (especially 16:13–14).

First, the promise is meant to alleviate the apostles' fear. They are about to lose Jesus, their teacher. But Jesus promises that the 'other Counsellor' he is sending is likewise a teacher; and a large aspect of his teaching ministry will be to prompt the apostles to remember what *Jesus* had taught. There is a guarantee of continuity in the content; and therefore the loss of Jesus as a human person they can touch and quiz and from whom they can learn is less traumatic than it might otherwise have been. Today when a pastor leaves a parish, or a professor an academic post, and a successor is appointed, the successor is not likely to agree with the former incumbent in every detail; and he is certainly not likely to spend a lot of time reminding his hearers of what the earlier pastor or professor said. But the Holy Spirit sees this as a prime objective: he will enable the disciples to recall what Jesus taught. This fact, if believed, could prove only reassuring to those first disciples.

Second, in teaching and reminding the disciples what Jesus taught, the Holy Spirit will explain things they did not understand at the time they were first uttered. This is a major theme in the fourth Gospel. A particularly telling example occurs in John 2. There John records the incident of the cleansing of the temple. 'What miraculous sign can you show us to prove your authority to do all this?' the Jews demand; to which Jesus replies, 'Destroy this temple, and I will raise it again in three days' (2:18–19). Not surprisingly, the Jews do not understand what Jesus means. They reply with mingled astonishment and scorn, 'It has taken forty-six years to build this temple, and you are going to raise it in three days?' John comments knowingly, 'But the temple he had spoken of was his body' (2:20–21). But then John adds one further comment which shows that the Jews were not alone in their misunderstanding: the disciples themselves did not at that time have any better idea what Jesus was saying. John comments, 'After he was raised from the dead, his disciples recalled what he had said. Then they believed the Scripture and the words that Jesus had spoken' (2:22).

The Farewell Discourse itself is testimony to the same phenomenon. Judging by the interruptions we have already examined, those of Thomas (14:5), Philip (14:8), and Judas (14:22), the thrust of Jesus' teaching was not clear to his disciples that night. They knew he was talking about his departure and about his death; it is doubtful if they put the two together. They certainly did not anticipate the resurrection; and they could not absorb the vision of a world-wide community of disciples set in antithesis to the world. But Jesus outlines these things anyway. What little they could take in would provide some comfort; and what they could neither remember nor understand would become doubly precious when, after the crucial events, they not only remembered what Jesus said, but by the Spirit's help understood its true significance; for men they would also recognize that Jesus told them these things in advance (see 14:29, discussed below).

Third, the Holy Spirit would teach those first disciples the significance not only of Jesus' words, but of the events themselves. The implications of the death/resurrection/exaltation of Jesus are staggering: how do these events relate to the Old Testament? Must believers in Jesus adhere to Old Testament law? Exactly what does the resurrection have to say about who Jesus is? Under what conditions may Gentiles be admitted to the community of believers? What did Jesus have in mind when he spoke of his personal return in the clouds of heaven? In the nature of the case, Jesus himself could not answer their questions; but the Holy Spirit would be there to instruct them. Even the most casual reading of the book of Acts reveals the enormous theological and conceptual barriers that the church had to cross as it struggled, sometimes with acute division of opinion, to come to grips with the full implications of Jesus' saving work. In those formative months and years, Jesus here assures his disciples, the Holy Spirit would lead his disciples into all truth.

In this sense the instruction of the Holy Spirit still had Jesus himself as its focus. It was the revelation of Jesus Christ that the Counsellor was completing. But this point is explicitly made in 16:12–14, and may better be proved in detail in a later chapter.

Fourth, there is an implicit but unavoidable suggestion that the community of believers will be around for some time – long enough to need the Spirit to remind them of Jesus' teaching and to instruct them further. The promise, in short, was for further revelation for an ongoing community, and in this sense the promise anticipated the New Testament canon.

By now it is clear that this first large bequest which Jesus leaves to his disciples is designed in the first place for the men with him in that upstairs room: in short, for the apostles in the narrow sense of the word. This is made clear by the promise that the Holy Spirit would *remind* them of what Jesus taught. Before the writing of the New Testament, such a promise could be relevant only to those who first heard what Jesus taught, and who could conceivably forget some of it These earliest witnesses were enabled, by the Spirit's help, to remember everything Jesus said, and make sense of the events of passion week and beyond. For this we must be very thankful.

Yet there is a legitimate secondary application which concerns Christians today. The Holy Spirit comes to live with us and be in us (14:17), too; and he helps us to call to mind, as we need them, the words of Scripture we have first learnt. This blessed promise should not prompt us to think that we need not bother to learn what Scripture teaches; for the Spirit can scarcely enable us to remember what we have never read nor heard. But this promise can remove the pressure of the fear of personal failure in our witness: the Spirit of God is perfectly able to help us remember what we need to know (cf. Matt. 10:19–20). The humblest saint with a growing knowledge of the Bible and the help of the Holy Spirit is able to stand up gently but tellingly to the most sophisticated of unbelievers. 'I have more insight than all my teachers,' the psalmist claims, 'for I meditate on your statutes' (Ps. 119:99).

2. *Peace,* This is the second large bequest which Jesus promises his followers in this passage. 'Peace I leave with you; my peace I give you. I do not give to you as the world gives. Do not let your hearts be troubled and do not be afraid' (14:27). A little later, Jesus promises the disciples his joy (15:11); but here and at the end of chapter 16, what he promises is his peace (16:33).

It is vital to recognize that the peace Jesus gives is not a kind of placid tranquillity which avoids all conflict. This is made particularly obvious by the second reference to peace in the Farewell Discourse. Jesus says, 'But a time is coming, and has come, when you will be scattered, each to his own home. You will leave me all alone . . . I have told you these things, so that in me you may have *peace*. In this world you will have trouble. But take heart! I have over-come the world' (16:32–33). Jesus himself is heading for the cross; yet he speaks of his peace. Similarly, the peace Jesus promises does not avoid trouble; it triumphs over it.

Nor is this peace to be confused with aloofness that is indifferent to injustice, corruption, idolatry, or some other sin. It is not simply 'feeling good' in some narcissistic way, nor is it some mystical sense of well-being detached from physical and spiritual realities. Although much loved by Eastern religions and promoted by certain modern cults, such 'peace' is both unrealistic and too fragile to compare with the robust versatility bound up with the biblical notion of peace.

To this day, Hebrew speakers greet each other with the traditional 'Shalom!'. The word is often rendered *peace*, but it is perhaps closer in meaning to 'well-being'. The idea of peace or well-being in the Scriptures can be usefully considered in three dimensions.

The first dimension of peace is vertical – peace with God. This is fundamental. In the Old Testament the promised Messiah is the Prince of Peace (Isa. 9:6). Moreover, for the Lord to give his people peace is virtually synonymous with turning his face towards them (Num. 6:26). God promises to establish an eternal covenant of peace with his people (Ezek. 37:26), one in which his 'David' will rule over them. In the New Testament Paul makes it clear that people who have been justified by faith in the Messiah, Jesus Christ, enjoy peace with God (Rom. 5:1). No peace is more fundamental than this peace. Because this is God's world and God's universe, no other peace is of ultimate value if we remain at enmity with him.

The second dimension of peace in the Scriptures is horizontal: it is peace with men. Just as our sin makes God our enemy, requiring that peace with God be established, so also our sin makes other people our enemies; and again, peace must be established. The solution Christ brings affords us both peace with God, and peace with men. Even the massive barrier between Jew and Gentile is overcome, according to the Epistle to the Ephesians, by making one new humanity in Christ Jesus, 'thus making peace' (Eph. 2:15). By reconciling both Jew and Gentile to God through the cross, Christ put to death their mutual hostility (Eph. 2:16).

The third dimension of peace is personal; and that is the peace primarily in view in John 14. This peace is a personal serenity which is not based on an ability to avoid troubles, but on a faith which transcends them. Paul appeals to the same principle of faith when he tells the chronic worrier to pray about his or her troubles, to pray with thanksgiving (Phil. 4:6). The concept of peace is important and much loved by Paul, as is made clear by his frequent use of the word. 'Now may the Lord of peace himself', he writes to the Thessalonians, 'give you peace at all times and in every way' (2 Thess. 3:16).

Although I have attempted to delineate the biblical notion of peace under these three dimensions, I cannot emphasize too strongly that the concept is nevertheless essentially wholistic. The biblical writers do not encourage us to aim for the best two out of three. A man cannot profitably pursue peace with God and with himself while still pursuing enmity with his brothers. Nor can he reasonably aim for peace with his brothers and with himself while ignoring the primacy of peace with God.

Theologically speaking, the reason the three dimensions of peace must be pursued together as parts of a whole lies in the fact that all shortages of peace are bound together with a common tie. That common tie is sin. Sin makes us enemies of God, enemies of others and enemies of ourselves. Sin alienates God from us, others from us, and alienates ourselves from ourselves (that is, it generates self-loathing, or artificial compensation, or profound feelings of guilt, or overt schizophrenia). Even in the external troubles which rob us of our peace, we detect the curse on mankind which is the entailment of the fall. The solution to this common malady is the cross and the resurrection. In this light it is difficult to believe that the repeated 'Peace be with you!' (20:19,21,26) with which Jesus greets his disciples after the resurrection is nothing but a commonplace greeting. Jesus in the Farewell Discourse promises his disciples peace; and after the resurrection he greets them in these triumphant words, 'Peace be with you!' Only in these two sets of passages is the word *peace* found in the fourth Gospel; and that is not mere coincidence.

The peace Jesus promises, then, is radical in the sense that it goes to the *radix* (root) of the problem. Jesus *leaves* his peace with his disciples: that is, Jesus' 'going away' via the cross is the step he takes to leave behind his peace.

Jesus gives peace in a way which the world cannot duplicate: 'I do not give to you as the world gives' (14:27). This is true both because of the distinctive *nature* of the peace Jesus gives, and because of the distinctive *way* in which Jesus gives it. The peace Jesus leaves his disciples is ultimately independent of outward, temporal circumstances. It turns on Christ's atoning crosswork, and on trust in the eternal God – not on health, power, prestige, new acquisitions or new excitement. The world's peace turns on transient variables that cannot engender stable peace.

But the way Jesus bequeaths this peace is distinctive, too. The world *wishes* peace on people. This is true not only in certain greetings (for example, *Shalom*, i.e., may well-being come your way; *Adieu*, i.e., we commit you and yours 'à Dieu' [= to God]), but also in the sincerest wishes of long-standing friends. Yet for all its wishing, the world cannot grant the gift of personal peace, but only wish it on someone. At most, it can achieve reconciliation between brothers or between nations; and even then the achievement often proves temporary. Christ, by contrast, bequeaths the gift of peace on all his followers, bestowing it as an essential part of the salvation he achieves for them. The cross wins peace with God. The forgiveness, restoration and healing which flow from this primary peace constitute the only adequate basis for peace with others, and for personal peace within ourselves.

'My peace.' The expression is stunning. It would be ludicrous on the lips of any other mortal. Could we imagine a Goethe or a Napoleon promising to leave his peace to his followers? Even from a Gandhi the expression would be hard to construe: how could Gandhi leave his own peace to his disciples? But the peace Jesus leaves to us is *his* peace in at least two ways. First, it is the peace which he himself provides; and second, it is part and parcel of the peace which he himself experienced during his mortal life. It is the product of his work on the cross; and the necessary soil for this peace to flourish is filial trust in and obedience towards God, virtues which he exemplified perfectly. 'My peace', Jesus says, 'I give you.'

So much of our restlessness and bitterness springs from our possessiveness, our desire for pre-eminence, our lust for recognition. Our love for self is so strong that it turns to hatred for others who do not give us what we think is our due. There is no peace where such sins flourish. Jesus betrayed no possessiveness. He desired his Father's glory and will, not personal pre-eminence and popular recognition. Far from loving his life, he gave it up for others – indeed, for others who did not begin to offer him what was his due. And so Jesus could speak of his peace.

But let us be frank: Jesus' peace is not something everyone wants. Sometimes that is because of misconceptions regarding the nature of that peace. To a person whose happiness seems to depend on excitement, the word *peace* may conjure up visions of rather dull old fogies rocking slowly by the dying embers of an ancient hearth. To a revolutionary, the word *peace* is nothing but a smug enjoyment of an evil *status quo*. Far sadder is the person who turns his back on Jesus' peace precisely because he realizes that the peace Jesus promises is full-orbed, involving God, other people, himself; that this peace presupposes a living relationship with Christ, and a walk of joyful submission to him; that this peace is no escape from reality but a courageous serenity even in the midst of troubles; that this peace involves dying daily to overgrown self-interest.

There are others, often humble folk, who came to know Christ as Lord and Saviour and who, by passing through enormous sloughs, came to rest on the stable peace Jesus gives. I think of a Christian police officer in Canada whose career was blighted for years by a senior officer who loathed his integrity. I think of Joni Eareckson. I think of a Christian couple in England whose first child was stillborn and whose second child died at the age of seven weeks. I think of a thoughtful Thai who, when he became a Christian, faced overt persecution from his close-knit Buddhist family. I think of a school teacher in Quebec who lost his job because he became a Christian. These people, and many like them, are living proof of the truth that Jesus gives peace. For some of them, the tears flowed freely and the nagging questions returned again and again; yet in each instance an essentially stable peace emerged as the product of faith.

The peace Jesus leaves his disciples is the effective antidote both to the troubled mind and to cowardice; for Jesus concludes his promise to send peace by enjoining, 'Do not let your hearts be troubled and do not be afraid' (14:27). With so rich a heritage to be enjoyed, it is positively sinful to worry and fret in a way which robs us of our peace. This is true whether the object of our fretting be the endless pressures of everyday life, the staggering hurdles that confront us more rarely, or the peculiar pressures applied to Christians. Trust in God, insists Jesus, and trust in me; and be assured that my departure entails large bequests for you, including the gift of my peace. The gift is yours: do not let your heart be troubled, and do not be afraid.

> Be still, my soul: the Lord is on thy side;
>   Bear patiently the cross of grief or pain;
> Leave to thy God to order and provide;

In every change He faithful will remain.
Be still, my soul: thy best, thy heavenly Friend
Through thorny ways leads to a joyful end.

Be still, my soul: thy God doth undertake
  To guide the future as He has the past
Thy hope, thy confidence let nothing shake;
  All now mysterious shall be bright at last.
Be still, my soul: the waves and winds will know
His voice who ruled them while He dwelt below.

Be still, my soul: the hour is hastening on
  When we shall be for ever with the Lord,
When disappointment, grief, and fear are gone,
  Sorrow forgot, love's purest joys restored.
Be still, my soul: when change and tears are past
All safe and blessed we shall meet it last.

Katharina von Schlegel (1697–?)
trans. Jane L. Borth

Jesus consoles his disciples, but he rebukes the shallowness of their self-interest

'You heard me say, "I am going away and I am coming back to you." If you loved me, you would be glad that I am going to the Father, for the Father is greater than I. I have told you now before it happens, so that when it does happen you will believe' (14:28–29).

Jesus returns to the theme which touched off much of his disciples' gloom, that is, his departure. He reminds them that they heard him say, 'I am going away and I am coming back to you' (14:28; cf. 14:3). But he now treats this topic in a manner quite new: he turns on the disciples and tells them their unhappiness at his impending departure is in reality an indication of how little they love him. 'If you loved me,' he says – implying they do not – 'you would be glad that I am going to the Father, for the Father is greater than I.'

It is difficult to understand what Jesus is saying until we come to grips with the last clause, 'the Father is greater than I.' The Jehovah's Witnesses, and others who have preserved the ancient Arian heresy (which denies the deity of Jesus Christ), cite this verse as proof of the validity of their position. The language itself is ambiguous and must be treated carefully. For example, I could truthfully insist, 'The president of the United States is greater than I.' But such a statement would not be taken by anyone to mean that the president is more of a human being than I, that he is ontologically on another plane. It simply means that he is greater in authority, position, rank, prestige, and in the honour accorded him. Similarly, for Jesus to say that the Father is greater than he is does not prove that the Father enjoys superiority at the ontological level, nor that Jesus is something of an inferior deity.

One might even argue that for Jesus to utter such a thought, and expect to be taken seriously, presupposes the essential oneness between Jesus and his Father. If I were to say, rather solemnly, that God is greater than I, I would be dressing up truth in ridiculous clothing, because the distance between God and me is so great that the comparison is in some respects ludicrous even while it is formally true. It would be far more ludicrous than for a common-or-garden slug to comment, 'The human being who owns this garden is greater than I.'

No interpretation of this passage is likely if it comes into conflict with other passages in the fourth Gospel which unambiguously affirm the deity of Jesus Christ.

The correct approach is to recall some of the emphases in John's Gospel on the person and work of Christ (discussed in chapter 2). We have learnt that the eternal Son of God emptied himself of his glory and came to birth as a human being – a dependent and obedient human being. The Father tells the Son what to do, not vice versa. The Father, in other words, is not only greater in the sense that the person with the greater authority is greater than the person with less, but also in the sense that the Father retains his glory, while the Son willingly sets his aside for the duration of his ministry (cf. 17:5: 'And now, Father, glorify me in your presence with the glory I had with you before the world began'). As C.K. Barren has finely put it, 'the Father is God sending and commanding, the Son is God sent and obedient. John's thought here is focused on the humiliation of the Son in his earthly life, a humiliation which now, in his death, reached both its climax and its end.'

In its context, the statement that the Father is greater than the Son functions as the *reason why*, if the disciples really loved Jesus, they would have been glad of his departure. The argument appears to be something like this: if they loved Jesus, then they would want what was best for him. Return to the Father would mean return to the glory he shared with the Father before the incarnation. His humiliation would be over, his triumph achieved, his reign as mediatorial king begun. Should not those who profess to love him rejoice with him at this prospect? Their gloom attests to their selfishness: they are miserable at the thought of losing him. But they evidence no joy – joy which would attest to their delight in what is best for him.

The sort of reaction Jesus might have hoped for is sometimes found at a truly Christian funeral. The loss of the beloved brother or sister in Christ, the cherished wife or husband, is bound to bring tears and wrenching emotional agony; yet at the same time, even the mourners delight to think about the joyful new vistas of the departed believer. Tears mingle with holy smiles: we do not 'grieve like the rest of men, who have no hope' (1 Thess. 4:13). Instead of this ambivalent joy and sorrow, however, Jesus' disciples reveal only self-interest.

Even as he rebukes them, Jesus consoles them. 'I have told you now before it happens,' he insists, 'so that when it does happen you will believe' (14:29; cf. 13:19). He has not told them of his impending departure via the cross in order to prolong their suffering as much as possible; he has told them in advance so that, when the crucial events unfold, the disciples will perceive that he knew what he was doing, and come to solid faith. They will not think that Jesus' enemies were too strong for him, or that he lost control of the situation even temporarily. As he insisted on another occasion, 'The reason my Father loves me is that I lay down my life – only to take it up again. No-one takes it from me, but I lay it down of my own accord. I have authority to lay it down and authority to take it up again' (10:17–18). According to Matthew, the scene of the arrest still finds Jesus saying the same sort of thing: 'Do you think I cannot call on my Father, and he will at once put at my disposal more than twelve legions of angels? But how then would the Scriptures be fulfilled that say it must happen in his way?' (Matt. 26:53–54). The disciples must recognize that in telling men of his departure he has their best interests at heart: he is preparing the way for them to come to a faith that could never again be shaken.

In short, Jesus in these verses (14:28–29) consoles his disciples, but rebukes their self-interest. He does something more: he rebukes *the shallowness* of their self-interest. Every reader of John's Gospel knows that the disciples' real self-interest lies in the one thing they devoutly wish to avoid: Jesus' departure. By his going away, Jesus accomplishes their redemption, becomes the way into the Father's presence, and bestows the Holy Spirit. All this they would miss, if their immediate and shallow self-interest were heeded.

The passage is steeped in irony. The disciples bemoan Jesus' departure, and thereby betray that they love themselves more than they love him; yet this very self-love, had its choices been granted, would not have gained what was truly in the interest of the disciples. Conversely, if the disciples had focused a little more attention on what the Lord Jesus wanted, on what was best for him, and a little less attention on their own grief, they would simultaneously have been fastening on to what was truly in their self-interest.

We ought not to be too hard on the disciples; for today we easily fall into similar traps. If we love self, we miss self's greatest good. If we die to self and genuinely seek the will of Jesus Christ, we discover in the end that his will is also our greatest good. To believe this – really to believe it – would eliminate many of our immature struggles, the death throes of an old nature that cries to assert itself. Its cries are deceitful: it appeals to self-interest, but it cannot possibly be in self's best interest, since it takes no account of the blessings found in Jesus Christ alone. The tragic irony of sinful self-love is that it gains nothing of real value for self, and loses everything. That is why Jesus, while consoling his disciples, rebukes the shallowness of their self-interest.

Jesus dies, but he dies as the sacrifice of a loving and obedient son, not as a pathetic or a guilty victim enmeshed in the tangles of fate or ensnared in the web of sin

'I will not speak with you much longer,' Jesus says, reminding them that the hour to which he has been pointing is almost upon them; 'for the prince of this world is coming. He has no hold on me, but the world must learn that I love the Father and that I do exactly what my Father has commanded me' (14:30–31).

The 'prince of this world' is the devil. His 'coming' in this context is equivalent to the coming of the 'hour' (12:27), the coming of the passion. The devil comes to oppose Jesus, to make him suffer and die. He has been inciting Judas to the most heinous betrayal of all time (6:70; 13:2,27), and now he comes to claim his prize. But even though the passion is a conflict between Jesus and Satan, there is no doubt about the outcome. The passion spells Satan's defeat; for Jesus earlier declared, 'Now is the time for judgment on this world; now the prince of this world will be driven out' (12:31).

In a similar vein, Jesus now says of Satan, 'He has no hold on me' (14:30). The words in the original literally rendered are, 'He has nothing in me'; though written in Greek, they echo a Hebrew idiom which means, 'He has no claim upon me.' The prince of this world could not possibly have a claim upon Jesus, for Jesus is not of this world. Jesus stands outside the devil's domain. Elsewhere in John's Gospel Jesus reveals he has no consciousness of sin (8:46); here he demonstrates the same fact by insisting that the devil has no claim on him. The claim the devil has on all other human beings is their sin, their guilt; but Jesus is guiltless.

Because he is without sin, because the prince of this world has no claim on him, therefore Jesus knows his impending passion is not his proper due. He goes to the cross, not because he himself is worthy of death, nor because of Satan's power, but because the Father has commanded him to go, and Jesus loves the Father so much he willingly discharges what the Father commands.

'The world', Jesus says, 'must learn that I love the Father and that I do exactly what my Father has commanded me' (14:31). His Father's command is to lay down his life, and to take it again (10:18). The passion is unfolding, and Jesus must die; but he dies as a loving and obedient son in voluntary self-sacrifice, not as a pathetic or guilty victim enmeshed in the tangles of fate or ensnared in the web of sin.

Christians today think of Jesus' death in its relation to themselves. We recognize that his death proves he loves us supremely. We are deeply moved when we sing:

> Alas! and did my Saviour bleed?
>   And did my Sovereign die?
> Would He devote that sacred head
>   For such a worm as I?
>
> Was it for sins that I had done
>   He groaned upon the tree?
> Amazing pity! Grace unknown!
>   And love beyond degree!
>
> *Isaac Watts (1674–1748)*

True, all true; but one-sided nevertheless. There is another element we dare not overlook when we think of the reasons why Jesus went to the cross. Jesus chose to die not only because he loved us, as wonderful as that thought is, but because he loved the Father and desired above all else to do his will.

We diminish the grandeur of the plan of redemption when we neglect this divine element. It is a mark of our egocentricity that we think the love of Christ has for its exclusive or even primary object human beings such as ourselves. This is not to minimize Christ's love for us; rather, it is to recognize the primacy of his love for the Father. The cross reveals how profoundly the eternal Son of God loves his Father and how utterly he obeys him and pleases him. Even in Gethsemane (Mk. 14), Jesus' anguish is spelt out in terms of coming to grips with his Father's will, not in terms of sacrificing himself for others.

Similarly, although it is true that the Father loved the world so much he sent his Son (3:16), this presupposes his love for that Son. The surprising thing is that the ministry, passion and triumph of the Son is not only the evidence of the Father's love *for us*, but the evidence of the Father's love *for his Son*, for it was by this means that the Father placed everything into his Son's hands. That is why the fourth Gospel says, 'The Father loves the Son and has placed everything in his hands' (3:35).

The Son's will is to please his Father, not just to save us; and the Father's will is to have all men honour the Son, not just to forgive us. To grasp these divine relationships in the drama of redemption is to humble our pride and heighten our sense of speechless privilege. To be saved and renewed, to be the recipients of new life, to be forgiven, all because we are caught up in the perfection of love among the Persons of the Godhead, is unutterably solemn, ecstatically wonderful.

To learn these truths not only prompts adoration; it calls forth imitation, Jesus' loving obedience towards his Father becomes the standard by which my loving obedience towards Jesus must be measured. That is why, in the next section, Jesus explicitly affirms, 'If you obey my commands, you will remain in my love, just as I have obeyed my Father's commands and remain in his love' (15:10).

Jesus departs, but he leaves his followers large bequests: the Holy Spirit, and Jesus' own peace.

Jesus consoles his disciples, but he rebukes the shallowness of their self-interest.

Jesus dies, but he dies as the sacrifice of a loving and obedient son, not as a pathetic or a guilty victim enmeshed in the tangles of fate or ensnared in the web of sin.

'Come now; let us leave.' So read the last words of John 14, according to the NIV. They interrupt the flow of the Farewell Discourse so dramatically that they have generated many explanations. Many scholars argue that such words indicate the end of a discourse, and that therefore the next two chapters are out of place. They theorize that either John 15 and 16 originally came *before* John 14, or that John 14 and John 15 – 16 are two reports of the same discourse which some insensitive editor slapped into the book back to back. Neither theory has much to commend it. There is no textual evidence for either of them; and against them is the fact that there is progression of thought from the beginning of chapter 14 to the end of chapter 16 (as this book attempts to show). Even if we do not adopt some theory of displacement, it must be admitted that the Greek grammar at the end of John 14 is difficult. My exposition follows the NIV, which in my judgment is most probably correct; but it is also possible to punctuate the text as follows: '[The devil] has no hold on me. But that the world may learn that I love the Father and that I do exactly what my Father has commanded me, come now, let us leave.' I see no reason to rule out this way of taking 14:30–31; but it is perhaps less likely than the punctuation of the NIV.

One British scholar, C.H. Dodd, takes the final words of 14:31 metaphorically as a rallying exhortation: 'The Ruler of this world is coming. He has no claim upon me; but to show the world that I love the Father, and do exactly as He commands, – up, let us march to meet him!' Such a rendering is not unattractive; but it faces severe difficulties. First, it is not obvious how chapters 15 and 16 readily follow such a rallying cry. Second, throughout the Farewell Discourse Jesus views the impending hour of the passion as the way he himself must take. It is his struggle, and his alone. It belongs to the disciples only in so far as they are troubled and confused over it. Third, the text does not say, 'let us march *to meet* Him!' It says rather, 'let us go *away from here*' or, in the language of the NIV, 'let us leave.'

On balance, it seems best to take the words, 'Come now; let us leave', as a pause in the Farewell Discourse during which Jesus and his disciples actually leave the upstairs room and begin their journey through the winding streets of Jerusalem, out through the gate and down the slope, across the brook Kidron and up the Mount of Olives. According to 18:1, they do not actually cross the Kidron until after Jesus has prayed the prayer of John 17.[3] But perhaps the content of chapters 15 to 17 was given between the time they left the upstairs room and the time they left the city wall behind and headed for the bottom of the valley. Could it be that local vineyards, or a sculpted vine on the city gate, called forth the vine imagery of John 15? Is it possible that the conversations of John 16:17–19 suggest that clumps of disciples engaged in whispered conversations as the narrow road constricted the group of twelve men and sometimes forced them to walk in smaller groups? Do the words,

'After Jesus said this, he *looked towards* heaven and prayed' (17:1) encourage the idea that Jesus and his men were outside, so that if eyes were raised they were lifted towards heaven and not towards the ceiling? It is difficult to be certain, and none of the evidence is conclusive; but I am more inclined to follow this sort of interpretation than any other.

5 (John 15:1–16)

Spiritual Intimacy with Jesus Christ

'I am the true vine and my Father the gardener. He cuts off every branch in me that bears no fruit, while every branch that does bear fruit he trims clean so that it will be even more fruitful, You are already clean because of the word I have spoken to you. Remain in me, and I will remain in you. No branch can bear fruit by itself; it must remain in the vine. Neither can you bear fruit unless you remain in me.

'I am the vine; you are the branches. If a man remains in me and I in him, he will bear much fruit; apart from me you can do nothing. If anyone does not remain in me, he is like a branch that is thrown away and withers; such branches are picked up, thrown into the fire and burned. If you remain in me and my words remain in you, ask whatever you wish, and it will be given you. This is to my Father's glory, that you bear much fruit, showing yourselves to be my disciples.

'As the Father has loved me, so have I loved you. Now remain in my love. If you obey my commands, you will remain in my love, just as I have obeyed my Father's commands and remain in his love. I have told you this so that my joy may be in you and that your joy may be complete. My command is this: Love each other as I have loved you. Greater love has no-one than this, that one lay down his life for his friends. You are my friends if you do what I command. I no longer call you servants, because a servant does not know his master's business. Instead, I have called you friends, for everything that I learned from my Father I have made known to you. You did not choose me, but I chose you to go and bear fruit – fruit that will last. Then the Father will give you whatever you ask in my name.'

Few passages in the Scripture are better known, at a superficial level, than the first few verses of John 15. Here Jesus claims to be the true vine. His Father is the gardener, and his followers are the branches. Fruitful branches are pruned to make them more fruitful; branches that bear no fruit are lopped off and burnt. The follower of Jesus must learn that, like a branch on a vine, he can be fruitful only as he 'remains' in Christ. 'Apart from me', Jesus insists, 'you can do nothing' (15:5). The believer who remains in the true vine is accorded the promise of effective prayer: 'If you remain in me and my words remain in you, ask whatever you wish, and it will be given you' (15:7). This is to the Father's glory. The thought is an echo of Jesus' earlier teaching in the Farewell Discourse (cf. 14:13–14).

Despite this isolated harking back to an earlier section, John 15 as a whole takes a substantial step forward. Jesus now focuses on the life, fruitfulness, prayer, witness and opposition his followers will experience in the interim period while he is away. There is a sustained development of these and similar themes all the way to 16:15.

The first verses of chapter 15 do not present us with a parable – at least, not with a parable like most of those recorded in the synoptic Gospels. There is no story, no plot. What we have is an extended metaphor without narrative – or, as C.K. Barren puts it, 'certain general observations on viticulture'. Be that as it may, Christians have long been attracted to these verses, both because they are profound and because they are perplexing.

They are profound in that they deal with certain deep realities in the Christian faith. Jesus is central to the passage: he himself is the *true* vine. The word *true* calls to mind other biblical passages that deal with vines. In particular, the Old Testament frequently calls the people of Israel God's vine (e.g. Ps. 80:8–16; Isa. 5:1–7; 27:2ff.; Jer. 2:21; 12:10–13; Ezek. 15:1–8; 19:10–14). Most of these passages stress how favoured and privileged this vine is, but also how corrupt. God 'looked for a crop of good grapes, but it yielded only bad fruit' (Isa. 5:2). God says, 'I had planted you like a choice vine of sound and reliable stock. How then did you turn against me into a corrupt, wild vine?' (Jer. 2:21). Now Jesus appears and declares himself to be the *true* vine.

As early as Psalm 80 there is an association between the vine and the Son of man; and perhaps there is an echo of that association in John 15. The real people of God are those who are branches in the true vine: this is what chapter 15 tells us. Just as Jesus' body is the true temple (John 2), and he is the true bread from heaven (John 6), the water that truly quenches thirst (John 4), the good shepherd (John 10), and the life which resurrects men from the dead (John 11), so is he the true vine. All of the shadows of the Old Testament disappear in the light of his substance (cf. Col. 2:17).

John 15 is profound and compelling for other reasons. It deals with the union between Christ and his followers, a union apart from which they can bear no fruit (15:4–5). Whatever is involved in this intimacy between Christ and Christians, it stands at the heart of spiritual vitality. So important is this fruit-bearing that every productive branch is pruned to make it more fruitful. This, too, is a focal point in the believer's experience. We do not walk the Christian way very far before painful pruning makes us cry out in self-pity and confusion; but the addition of a little more time helps us see that the heavenly gardener knows what he is about, and acknowledge with gratitude the greater fruitfulness that has come into our lives. Small wonder that John 15 has been for many centuries a favourite passage among believers.

But the passage is as perplexing as it is profound. Exactly what kind of fruit are we expected to bear? Does any believer really enjoy the extravagant prayer promises in verses 7 and 8? Exactly what does 'remaining in Christ' really mean? Above all, how is it that branches are said to be in this vine, yet fruitless? And how can these branches be cut off and destroyed?

I do not propose to answer these questions directly. However, the next verses in the chapter, verses 9–16, deal with a question which stands behind all the others; and if we come to grips with that one, the others will fit into place. John 15:9–16 deals with the nature of the intimacy between Jesus and the believer, between the vine and the branch. I take it to be Jesus' own exposition of the extended metaphor he has just used. The numerous parallels between 15:1–8 and 15:9–16 seem to suggest this: the continued emphasis on 'remaining', the references to bearing fruit, the sense of privilege in belonging to the vine/Jesus, the culmination of both sections in the large promises concerning prayer. These are but a few of the parallels we shall observe; and in coming to grips with these parallels, we shall discover that the exposition of

15:9–16 is simultaneously the exposition of the main themes of 15:1–8, and an answer to the perplexities of the latter.

John 15:8–16 insists on five things concerning the nature of the intimacy between Jesus and the believer.

The intimacy between Jesus Christ and the believer is an intimacy paralleled in some respects by the intimacy between Jesus and his Father

'As the Father has loved me, so have I loved you. Now remain in my love. If you obey my commands, you will remain in my love, just as I have obeyed my Father's commands and remain in his love. I have told you this so that my joy may be in you and that your joy may be complete' (15:9–11). There are three common elements:

1. As Jesus is the object of the Father's love, so the believer is the object of Jesus' love. This is explicitly stated in the text: 'As the Father has loved me, so have I loved you' (15:9*a*).

If in the first verse of this Gospel we read that the Word was God, we read in the same verse that the Word was with God; and the peculiar expression used means the Word was in the presence of God. From all eternity past this was so; and for all that 'time' the Father loved the Son. John presupposes this when he tells us that God is love (1 John 4:8). A God who has always lived in solitary seclusion cannot realistically be described as a loving God; but a God who exists as one God in three Persons may indeed be exercising profound love. Jesus makes explicit that the Father loved him before the creation of the world (17:24). This love of the Father for the Son is again presupposed by the assumed contrast in the words, 'For God so loved the world that he gave his one and only Son . . .' (3:16).

Paul similarly presupposes the eternal love of the Father for the Son when he argues, 'He who did not spare his own Son, but gave him up for us all – how will he not also, along with him, graciously give us all things?' (Rom. 8:32). God has already given his best gift, his most cherished gift; and that gift is the Son he loves.

This love of the Father for the Son is not restricted to the Son's pre-incarnate state. Twice John's Gospel tells us that the Father loves the Son (3:35; 5:20); and both times the context shows that it is Jesus Christ the incarnate Son who is in view. According to the synoptic Gospels, Jesus began his public ministry when he was baptized by John the Baptist, only to hear the silence of heaven broken by the Father's public declaration, 'You are my Son, whom I love; with you I am well pleased' (Mark 1:11 and parallels). The transfiguration brought another public testimony of the Father's love: 'This is my Son, whom I love. Listen to him!' (Mark 9:7 and parallels).

And now we read Jesus' utterly amazing words, 'As the Father has loved me, so have I loved you' (15:9a). We have already discovered that the Son loves the Father, and that our salvation springs from Jesus' desire to please his Father (14:30–31, and the fourth chapter of this book); but to be told as well that Jesus loves us with the same love by which the Father loves him is astounding.

> Surely Thy sweet and wondrous love
>   Shall measure all my days;
> And as it never shall remove,
>   So neither shall my praise.
>
> *George Herbert (1593–1632)*

There is a touch of eternity built into such love. Small wonder Jesus says, a few verses on, 'You did not choose me, but I chose you . . .' (15:16).

In some sense, then, the Son is the mediator of the Father's love to us; but we must not think that the Father himself fails to love us. Quite the contrary: in the High Priestly prayer, Jesus says to his Father, 'You sent me and have loved them even as you have loved me' (17:23). Nevertheless, for Jesus to say, 'As the Father has loved me, so have I loved you' (15:9*a*), prompts us to reflect and marvel at the thought that believers enjoy something of the intimacy with Jesus that Jesus enjoys with his Father. The Father is the gardener who cherishes the vine; the vine cherishes the branches. Not that the gardener has no regard for the branches and focuses all attention exclusively on the vine; but the branches have no place in the garden and in the gardener's affection unless they are nurtured by the vine. It is in this sense that the Son is the mediator of the Father's love.

2. As Jesus remains in his Father's love by means of obedience, so the believer must remain in Jesus' love by means of obedience. 'Now remain in my love', Jesus insists. 'If you obey my commands, you will remain in my love, just as I have obeyed my Father's commands and remain in his love' (15:9*b*–10).

Although Jesus is the object of his Father's love, he does not for this reason rest on his laurels and bask in the love he enjoys, oblivious to the responsibilities which the enjoyment of another's love brings. Rather, Jesus remains in his Father's love by means of obedience to his Father's commands. The Father does not leave Jesus alone, because Jesus always does what pleases him (8:29). We have already considered in detail how the Son stands with his Father, with respect to men, in revelation and authority, while standing with men, with respect to the Father, in submission and dependence (see p. 31); and now we see afresh the emphasis on Jesus' submission to the will of his Father.

This submission is a model for believers. What an example the Scriptures set before us: even the Son of God learnt obedience through suffering. Here is no isolated deity who cannot be touched with the feeling of our temptations. Jesus knows what it is to obey commands. For this reason his injunction carries with it not only the authority of the Godhead, but the authority of personal experience: 'If you obey my commands, you will remain in my love, just as I have obeyed my Father's commands and remain in his love' (15:10).

Earlier, Jesus taught, 'If you love me, you will obey what I command' (14:15): the reality of the disciples' profound love is to be proved by their obedience. But now the disciples' obedience is not presented as the evidence of their love, but as the means for remaining in Jesus' love.

We must exercise particular care in observing what the text does *not* say. Jesus does not suggest that our obedience somehow earns his love, nor that his love is so sullen and miserly that it must be wrenched from him by a kind of moral bribery. Were this the case, the divine love would not be prior; and we know that it is (3:16; cf. 1 John 4:10–11).

Perhaps we can most easily understand what Jesus means by reflecting on some New Testament examples. Ananias and Sapphira were baptized believers; yet because of their deceit before the Holy Spirit, they were killed (Acts 5). They did not remain in Jesus' love. Being killed, of course, does not in itself prove that they did not remain in Jesus' love: after all, Stephen too was killed (Acts 7). But Stephen died a martyr's death; Ananias and Sapphira died as the result of divine judicial action.

We may think of those Corinthians who approached the Lord's Supper in an unworthy manner and fell ill as a result. Some of them died (1 Cor. 11): they did not remain in Jesus' love. John refers to professing believers who run ahead and do not remain in the teaching of Christ: such people, John insists, do not have God (2 John 9). Jude echoes the teachings of his exalted half-brother when he pens the words, 'Keep yourselves in God's love' (Jude 21).

What must be noticed in these and other biblical passages that treat the love of God or the love of Jesus is that there is a broad spectrum of ideas associated with God's love; and this spectrum changes according to the context. The Bible insists on God's wrath against all men, a wrath grounded in his holy nature; yet it insists on God's love for all men, sending his Son and inviting them to come to him. The Bible also speaks of God's love in a narrower sense: he chooses a Jacob above an Esau, a David instead of a Saul, an entire people for the praise of his glorious grace.[4] It is often illegitimate to transfer the associations of one passage on God's love to some other passage; and it is always illegitimate to use the associations of one passage to disallow those of another passage.

In the context of John 15, Jesus is talking about his *love for his disciples*, not how they became his disciples. Being a disciple, being an intimate of Jesus, entails certain responsibilities. For a start, it requires obedience: only obedience ensures that the disciple will remain in Jesus' love. Similarly, in the extended vine metaphor of the preceding verses, no branch can bear fruit unless it remains in the vine; and the branch that does not bear fruit is lopped off and burnt. Where there is growth and fruit-bearing by virtue of connection with the vine, there, too, is life; where there is neither growth nor fruit-bearing, there is no life. In terms of discipleship, Jesus explains the metaphor by saying, 'This is to my Father's glory, that you bear much fruit, *showing yourself to be my disciples*' (15:8).[5]

The question must then be squarely faced: can true believers lose their salvation, or not? Can a person be a branch in the vine, and then subsequently be cast off and destroyed?

This question is an important one; but it is important only for those who have a high view of Scripture and who therefore think that the statements of the Bible ultimately can be reconciled with one another. If someone does not share this perspective, there is nothing to prevent him from supposing that one biblical book teaches one thing and another biblical book teaches a contradictory thing. He might even suppose that some of the biblical authors were so confused that they contradicted themselves.

The person with a high view of Scripture, however, tries to synthesize passages which seem to say that a believer cannot fall completely away with other passages which seem to say that a believer can indeed be utterly rejected; he believes one God of truth stands behind both sets of passages. On the one hand, he recalls Jesus' words, 'And this is the will of him who sent me, that I shall lose none of all that he has given me, but raise them up at the last day' (6:39); and again, 'My sheep listen to my voice; I know them, and they follow me. I give them eternal life, and they shall never perish; no-one can snatch them out of my hand' (10:27–28). He remembers that Paul is confident 'that he who began a good work in you will carry it on to completion until the day of Christ

Jesus' (Phil. 1:6). On the other hand, he reads here of branches in Christ that bear no fruit and are cut off; and he wonders how he can possibly deal fairly and honestly with all the evidence.

This is not the place to undertake a full-scale exploration of the subject; but perhaps it would be helpful to give some pointers to what I judge to be a solution. False solutions abound: some, for example, suggest that the person who bears no fruit is cast off and burnt *as a branch* but not as a believer. Such a 'solution' too rigidly distinguishes between the metaphor and that which the metaphor represents. Others suggest that the passage as a whole does not deal with Christians, but with Jews who fail to accept Jesus as the true Messiah. The vine metaphor becomes akin to Paul's metaphor of the olive tree in Romans 11, with Jewish branches being broken off and Gentile branches being grafted in. But John 15 does not speak of 'grafting' at all. The context does not raise the Jew/Gentile distinction, but speaks of branches in *Christ* that are cut off. Christians (whether Jew or Gentile) are in view.

A genuine resolution of this problem will begin with the recognition that our theology of conversion is probably inadequate. We are inclined to think that once a person has made a decision, he is saved, and that is that. There is some biblical evidence to support this view: a person who has faith in Jesus Christ has indeed come to experience the new birth (John 3), and the simple instruction to the Philippian jailer should not be freighted down with endless qualifications (Acts 16). Nevertheless, there is much biblical evidence to suggest that a person's spiritual condition should be addressed more phenomenologically than ontologically: that is, more according to his behaviour and responses than according to what is going on in his very being. True conversion in the Scripture presupposes some genuine change in what a man truly is; but this does not stop the biblical writers from dealing with what a man says and does. Only God can assess the heart; you and I are left to assess words and deeds.

For example, in the parable of the sower (Mark 4 and parallels), Jesus describes four different types of soil. Only one, the 'good' soil, bears fruit (in various yields). Of the other three soils, two produce a living plant: the shallow soil on rocky places, and the soil infested with thorns. The hard-packed path bears nothing, because the birds (= devil) come and snatch the seed away; but the other two poor soils do begin to produce something of promise. Indeed, the seed planted in shallow soil seems at first to be the most promising of the lot. Jesus' description is telling: 'Others, like seed sown on rocky places, hear the word and at once receive it with joy. But since they have no root, they last only a short time. When trouble or persecution comes because of the word, they quickly fall away' (Mark 4:16–17). In short, genuine conversion is not measured by the hasty decision but by the long-range fruitfulness.

The apostle John adopts the same perspective when discussing certain antichrists who had left the church and were propagating false teaching and low morals. How should they be viewed, since they, too, had been baptized and had at one time enjoyed communion with true believers? Writes John, 'They went out from us, but they did not really belong to us. For if they had belonged to us, they would have remained with us; but their going showed that none of them belonged to us' (1 John 2:19). In other words, John unambiguously insists that their very apostasy proves they were never true believers. They turned away from the truth, they abandoned the fellowship in which they had participated, they rejected the stands they had once taken; but even so,

John insists, they could not have been true believers or
else they would not have done such things.

True faith holds fast till the end. The writer to the
Hebrews says as much, using an interesting combina-
tion of verb tenses: 'We have come to share in Christ if
we hold firmly till the end the confidence we had at first'
(Heb. 3:14). As John says, 'Whoever continues in the
teaching has both the Father and the Son' (2 John 9).

To perceive these things is also to see how close a person may come to salvation without ever having the root
of the matter within him. A person may believe, in the
sense that he has come to thorough assent; he may pass
all tests a discerning church may offer, and be baptized;
he may become a disciple, a follower of Jesus in the
sense that he adheres (as far as anyone can see) to Jesus'
teachings; he may give his testimony and taste something of new stirrings for holiness because of the company he is keeping. To all who are limited by the
phenomenological, that person is a Christian, a brother.
He is a branch; he is a seed that is sprouting and growing. But if at that point he rejects the truth, remains fruitless, or wilts before opposition, the biblical writers I
have cited concur in this: he could not possibly have
been a true believer in the first place. John 2:23–25 makes
it clear that a person can in some sense put his trust in
Jesus, and yet not be a true believer. Judas Iscariot was
accepted by the Twelve, and none suspected his traitor-
ous defection; but the final verdict is that it would have
been better for him if he had never been born.

These are sombre thoughts; but they serve to emphasize the thrust of Jesus' argument: the believer is responsible for remaining in Jesus' love, and he accomplishes
this by means of obedience. This does not suggest
perfect obedience: the fruit-bearing branch still needs to
be trimmed and pruned, and will continue to require

such treatment until Jesus comes again. Nor should we be so arrogant as to think we are wise enough and committed enough to keep ourselves: those who with much striving remain in Jesus' love discover that Jesus himself is keeping them. In the words of Paul, they work out their own salvation only to learn that God is working in them to will and to act according to his good purpose (Phil. 2:13). But when all qualifications are carefully registered, the full force of Jesus' teaching in John 15 must burn its message on our minds: as Jesus remains in his Father's love by means of obedience, so the believer must remain in Jesus' love by means of obedience. That is what it means to remain in the vine; that is what intimacy with Jesus entails. Failure at this point calls in question the validity of our commitment to Jesus Christ.

There is a danger in stressing this parallel between our intimacy with Jesus and his intimacy with the Father. The danger is that the responsibility to remain in Jesus' love can sound so severe, so humourless, so stark, as to evoke fearful and even frenzied compliance, but not love and not joy. Perhaps it is because he recognizes this danger that Jesus offers a third element in the parallel:

3. *As Jesus' supreme joy is in this relationship of obedience to the Father, so the Christian's supreme joy lies in his relationship of obedience to the Son.* 'I have told you this', says Jesus, referring to the parallel he has already drawn concerning obedience, 'so that my joy may be in you and that your joy may be complete' (15:11).

This raises Jesus' obedience to his Father to a new and lofty plane. Jesus delights to do his Father's will; his joy depends on pleasing his Father. So profound and unwavering is his love for the Father that what he wants most is to please him; and to please the Father gives the Son the deepest joy and satisfaction. Jesus recognizes this is true of himself; and he wants this his joy to be shared by his followers. They will drink deeply of his joy if they imitate his obedience. The ultimate draught is 'complete joy', which presupposes complete and unqualified obedience.

The joy Jesus promises is therefore not merely some cheap glow which depends on outward circumstances. It is the profound delight of the godly person whose 'delight is in the law of the LORD' (Ps. 1:2), the sublime gladness of whole-hearted obedience. Every Christian who has travelled any distance on his pilgrimage knows this to be so. His deepest joy springs from periods in his life when he obeys Christ with unreserved commitment. When some difficult decision with complex moral over-tones thrusts itself upon him, and he rejects various sinewy trails in favour of an unqualified adherence to the highest path for Jesus' sake, then he experiences joy that leaves him speechless.

No-one is more miserable than the Christian who for a time hedges in his obedience. He does not love sin enough to enjoy its pleasures, and he does not love Christ enough to relish holiness. He perceives that his rebellion is iniquitous, but obedience seems distasteful. He does not feel at home any longer in the world, but the memory of his past associations and the tantalizing lyrics of his old music prevent him from singing with the saints. He is a man most to be pitied; and he cannot for ever remain ambivalent.

Jesus experienced the joy of a completely fruitful life because he was obedient to his Father; and he desires that his followers share to the greatest extent that same fruitful joy by being utterly obedient to him.

This is the third way in which the intimacy between Jesus Christ and the believer parallels the intimacy between Jesus and his Father. We must not think this list is exhaustive: for instance, after the resurrection, Jesus draws another parallel by telling his disciples, 'As the Father has sent me, I am sending you' (20:21). On the other hand, we must not think that the list of parallels is endless. In the final evaluation, Jesus is unique. Perfectly God and perfectly man, he alone is the vine; we are the branches.

The intimacy between the believer and Jesus Christ is an intimacy which, far from being individualistic, is shared within the warmth of love for other believers – a love that imitates Christ's love for us

'My command is this: Love each other as I have loved you. Greater love has no-one than this, that one lay down his life for his friends' (15:12–13).

Formally, the connection between these two verses and what precedes is the word *command*. Jesus' disciples are to experience joy by obeying his commands, thereby remaining in his love. These commands are now sum-marized in one command, the command to love one another, even to the point of voluntarily laying down one's life for a friend.

Earlier that evening, Jesus had given his 'new com-mandment': 'A new commandment I give you: Love one another. As I have loved you, so you must love one another. All men will know that you are my disciples if you love one another' (13:34–35). This command is new in several ways. It is new in that it invokes a new stan-dard: 'as I have loved you.' It is for ever new in that it comes to us again and again in our need, new in the same way that God's mercies are new every morning:

'for though doctrinal Christianity is always old, experimental Christianity is always new' (R. Candlish). But above all it is new in that love is declared by Jesus to be the distinguishing mark of Christians in this new age, the identifying characteristic of true believers before a watching world.

But why does Jesus return to that theme here? Apart from the formal connection of the word *command*, why should the love command be raised afresh in this context? There are probably several reasons. It is good psychology to nail down general remarks about obedience to Jesus' commands to one specific and central command. In addition, love itself may well be construed as part of the fruit of the vine. (On the nature of the fruit in Jn. 15 I shall say more later in this chapter.) Moreover, Jesus presented his metaphor of the vine to the assembled disciples as a group. He addressed them in the plural: You – all of you – are the branches. In so doing he anticipated the development in Paul of a full-blown theology of unity in diversity: the body is one, but has many members. The vine is one, but has many branches.

Certainly in a context which discusses the intimacy between the believer and Jesus Christ it is helpful to be reminded that this intimacy is not an exclusivistic, maneuvering, or selfish relationship. It is a shared intimacy, shared with brothers and sisters in the faith, shared within the warmth of love that looks to Christ's love for its standard.

This disqualifies any cheap spiritual glow which does not boast the rigour of deep love among believers. Sad to tell, we Christians are ever capable of describing the delights of love in the new heaven and the new earth while still hoarding our resentments, animosities and bitterness down here. As one wag has put it:

> To live above with those you love –
>   Undiluted glory!
> To live below with those you know –
>   Quite another story.

In the Western world we often try to compensate for our failures in this regard by constructing a pseudo-Christian model of rugged spiritual individualism. The believer who pictures himself from such a vantage-point may suppose he enjoys a special intimacy with Jesus; but Jesus himself insists that the intimacy between himself and one of his followers is an intimacy shared within the framework of love for other Christians.

A Puritan pastor has it right:

> He wants not friends that hath Thy love,
>   And may converse and walk with Thee,
> And with Thy saints here and above,
>   With whom for ever I must be.
>
> In the communion of the saints
>   Is wisdom, safety and delight;
> And, when my bean declines and faints,
>   It's raisèd by their heat and light.
>
> *Richard Baxter (1615–91)*

Some object that this passage narrows love down too much. Does not Jesus in the Sermon on the Mount (Matt. 5 to 7) enjoin love *for enemies* upon his disciples? Why, then, does this passage say that no-one can have greater love than this, that one lay down his life *for his friends*?

One must not suppose that in the fourth Gospel God does not love the world (3:16). Elsewhere the New Testament makes it clear that Jesus died for sinners, for God's enemies (Rom. 5:7–10). Nevertheless the love the

Father shows the world – in the loving mission of the
Son – results in the formation of a group of disciples
which is, in some respects, set over against the world
(15:18ff.). Within that group, Jesus pours out his special
love and enables them to be caught up into the love
shared in the Godhead. Moreover, in this context Jesus is
not primarily interested in developing his followers'
attitudes *vis-à-vis* the world: rather, he wishes to establish the identity and distinctive features of his disciples,
of his church.

It is remarkable that Jesus' last extended discourse
before the cross spends so much time exhorting the disciples to love one another and to obey Jesus' commands,
and so little time enjoining them to doctrinal purity. This
is not to suggest that doctrinal purity is of indifferent
significance: many passages insist that turning away
from Christ can be grounded as well in false doctrine as
in moral declension or lovelessness. But in the Farewell
Discourse, doctrine is presented with pastoral concern
as grounds for encouragement and faith, rather than as
the minimum content which must be absorbed to ward
off apostasy.

The believer who hungers for deep intimacy with
Jesus Christ must follow this new command. It is not
easy. The unlovely ones in the brotherhood bring out the
worst in me. The winners get on my nerves. The gossips
and the arrogant, the immature and the silly, conspire to
drain my reserve. But the answer is to remember that the
branch can do nothing apart from the vine, and that
Jesus himself loved his friends, his unlovely, whining,
gossipy, arrogant, immature and silly friends, enough to
die for them.

The intimacy between the believer and Jesus Christ is an intimacy honoured by the noun *friendship* but it is a friendship carefully qualified

Jesus now picks up on the word *friends*. The disciples can exhibit no greater love than this, that they lay down their lives for their friends. But Jesus himself was about to become the supreme standard: he would lay down his life for his friends in just a few short hours. Yet Jesus' relation to his friends is not quite the same as their relation to one another, for Jesus now goes on to say, 'You are my friends if you do what I command. I no longer call you servants, because a servant does not know his master's business. Instead, I have called you friends, for everything that I learned from my Father I have made known to you' (15:14–15).

It is crucial to the understanding of this passage to note that the disciples are said to be Jesus' friends, but Jesus is not said to be their friend. In fact, nowhere in Scripture is either the Father or the Lord Jesus ever said to be the friend of anyone. Abraham may be called the friend of God (Isa. 41:8), but the Scriptures do not call God the friend of Abraham. On one occasion Jesus apparently uses the expression 'my friends' rather loosely (Luke 12.4); but nowhere is this reciprocated.

At first glance this is rather strange, the more so in the light of Christian hymnody. We sing with appreciation such hymns as this:

> I've found a Friend, O such a Friend!
>   He loved me ere I knew Him;
> He drew me with the cords of love,
>   And thus He bound me to Him;

And round my heart still closely twine
  Those ties which naught can sever,
For I am His, and He is mine,
  For ever and for ever.

James Grindlay Small (1817–88)

or again:

What a Friend we have in Jesus,
  All our sins and griefs to bear!
What a privilege to carry
  Everything to God in prayer!

Joseph M. Scriven (1820–86)

or again:

Jesus! What a Friend for sinners!
  Jesus! Lover of my soul;
Friends may fail me, foes assail me,
  He, my Saviour, makes me whole.

J. Wilbur Chapman (1859–1918)

All of these hymns express true ideas, and I do not hesitate to sing them. After all, the Scriptures never present Jesus as *un*friend. If friendship is measured purely by love poured out, then Jesus is the greatest friend.

Yet the fact remains that the Scriptures never refer to him by the noun *friend*. A moment's reflection reveals why. The word *friend* can conjure up so reciprocal a relationship of affection that it would badly distort and misrepresent the relationship that actually exists between Jesus and his followers. In short, there is a danger of a chummy view of friendship which neither embraces real love nor preserves the fundamental distinction between Jesus and those he redeems.

When Jesus calls his followers *friends* in this passage, therefore, it is a friendship carefully qualified. 'You are my friends if you do what I command' (15:14): clearly, this friendship cannot be reciprocal! To be a friend of Jesus is at this point indistinguishable from remaining in Jesus' love: both turn on obedience. Yet Jesus insists this is not the same as servanthood or slavery. A servant, like this 'friend', must do what he is told; but the servant operates in the dark, as it were, carrying out directions blindly, whereas the friend has been let in on the master's business and understands the significance of the commands.

Suppose a despotic monarch were to order his chauffeur to bring his car around. The chauffeur would go and do it, without asking for a detailed explanation, an itinerary, or the nature of the business or pleasure that might prompt this excursion. But were the dictator to tell a close friend to fetch the car, the friend might well venture a few questions. The friend would not be disposed to tell the monarch what to do; but he might well be let in on the business.

The distinction Jesus draws between a servant and a friend is not the distinction between obeying and not obeying, but the distinction between not understanding and understanding. The friend is let in on what is going on. This understanding stems not from superior intelligence or trained mental acuity, but from revelation graciously bestowed: Jesus himself makes known to his friends everything that he has learnt from his Father.

In one sense, then, Christians continue to be slaves of Jesus Christ, inasmuch as they are pledged to obey him. Paul continues to refer to himself in this way (e.g. Rom. 1:1). At the same time, Christians are in another sense no longer slaves but friends, inasmuch as they have received the wonderful privilege of being taught something of the sweep of God's plan of redemption. Paul uses a similar contrast. Although he calls himself a slave, yet he also points out that believers are no longer slaves but sons, inasmuch as they have left behind the covenant which treated them like children and come under the covenant which enables them to participate in the delights of their promised inheritance (Gal. 4:1–7).

The text asks of the reader, 'Are you a friend of Jesus?' The answer must not come back in vague terms: 'I consider myself a friend of Jesus', or 'I try to be', or the like. The friend of Jesus is characterized by two things: he does what Jesus commands, and he understands the revelation of God which Jesus has graciously revealed.

How does this relate to the extended metaphor of the vine at the beginning of the chapter? In part, it is another way of explaining what it means for the branch to remain in the vine, or for the disciple to remain in Jesus Christ. But there may be something more. These verses about friends of Jesus preserve a *distinction* between Jesus and his followers; and perhaps branches too need to be reminded on occasion that they themselves are not the vine. The vine supports and nourishes the branches and enables them to bear fruit; but the relationship is not exactly reciprocal.

The intimacy between believers and Jesus Christ is a fruitful intimacy grounded ultimately not in our choice of Christ but in Christ's choice of us

Jesus is explicit: 'You did not choose me, but I chose you to go and bear fruit – fruit that will last' (15:16a). The 'I' is emphatic in the original.

There is a strong emphasis on divine election in John's Gospel. In trying to come to grips with this emphasis, whether here or elsewhere in the canon, three boundary observations eliminate much harmful speculation: (1) God is absolutely sovereign, according to the Scriptures, but his sovereignty never reduces man to the status of a robot or a puppet. Man's choices are significant. (2) Man is responsible before God for all he is and does and has; but his responsibility never makes God contingent. (3) Theological errors in this extremely complex area of doctrine can largely be avoided if one restricts oneself to deductions which the biblical authors themselves offer, and to careful observation of how God's sovereignty and man's responsibility function in the Scripture. For instance, the biblical writers never deduce from a man's choice that God is sovereign in all areas *except* the moral areas of life (as, for instance, the rabbis and Philo do); so we should avoid such deductions also.

If we can get beyond the place where we are fighting over the meaning of election but failing to observe how election functions in holy writ,[6] we shall begin to notice how often in John's Gospel election is introduced just at the point where human arrogance may need a gentle lesson in humility (e.g. 6:70; 13:18). So it is here. The followers of Jesus are being introduced to spiritual fruitfulness, they are being designated friends of Jesus, they are the objects of Jesus' special love: it is enough to turn anyone's head. But then, just to hold things in perspective, Jesus reminds his men, 'You did not choose me, but I chose you to go and bear fruit – fruit that will last.'

This truth is of overwhelming importance if we hope to escape the puffy spiritual arrogance that talks almost as if Jesus has been blessed by our presence, as if we have done him a favour by choosing to trust him. I do not doubt for a moment that men are responsible to repent and believe; but it is salutary to recognize that no believer will have legitimate grounds for claiming, throughout all eternity, that he made it and his neighbour did not because he made the right choice. One of the songs that will surely be sung for ever around the throne is this one:

> I sought the Lord, and afterward I knew
> He moved my soul to seek Him, seeking me;
> It was not I that found, O Saviour true;
> No, I was found of Thee.
>
> Thou didst reach forth Thy hand and mine enfold;
> I walked and sank not on the storm-vexed sea;
> 'Twas not so much that I on Thee took hold,
> As Thou, dear Lord, on me.
>
> I find, I walk, I love; but O the whole
> Of love is but my answer, Lord, to Thee!
> For Thou wert long beforehand with my soul;
> Always Thou lovedst me.

Anon.

Sometimes we are quicker to acknowledge biblical truth in our hymns than in our prose. Would any Christian balk at singing, 'Loved with everlasting love, Led by grace that love to know'?

An intimacy with Jesus that is ultimately grounded in his choice of us yields fruit that lasts. Now we no longer hear of branches that are cut off and destroyed; we hear rather of boughs that bear fruit – real fruit – which lasts and thereby proves the authenticity of the branch.

The intimacy between the believer and Jesus Christ is an intimacy whose fruit is the result of prayer under Christ's Lordship

This is probably a clarification of the result that springs from Jesus' choice of his people: 'the Father will give you whatever you ask in my name' (15:16b). Such a large prayer promise is enunciated in 14:13–14 and again at the end of the vine imagery (15:7–8). What does it mean?

Most Christians are fairly sure what it does *not* mean. To ask in Jesus' name is not to use his name like some magical abracadabra or Aladdin's lamp. Jesus' name is not an occult formula given to satiate our every whim. It will not provide me with a gold-plated limousine (and if it did, it would also have to provide the fuel!)

But what does praying in Jesus' name mean? At very least, prayer in Jesus' name is: (1) prayer in accord with all that name stands for; (2) prayer that seeks God's glory (cf. 15:8); and (3) prayer which is consciously uttered under Christ's Lordship, much as baptism in Jesus' name signifies in part coming under Christ's Lordship. Hence John writes, 'This is the assurance we have in approaching God: that if we ask anything *according to his will*, he hears us' (1 John 5:14). 'According to his will' in this context is not very different from 'in my name'.

This is not a tawdry promise which is nothing but a pious way of saying *que sera, sera*. It is a powerful and specific promise which we badly need to learn to use a little better.

About twenty years ago I began one summer to spend Monday evenings in prayer with another Christian, a minister who was a little older than I. We arranged to get together at whatever time we were both free; and sometimes we prayed only for an hour or so, and sometimes for many hours, long into the night. After several weeks of this new experience, I began to feel a trifle bored. It was not so much that I resented praying, or felt that I was wasting time: quite the opposite, I was rather pleased with myself for taking the commitment on. Yet somehow I did not feel as if I were truly doing business with God, as if I were bearing the fruit I should be bearing.

The next week my minister friend changed the approach. In retrospect, I am quite sure he was trying to tutor me in the rudiments of praying. He suggested that instead of praying indiscriminately for all and sundry, we would that week seek to discover what we should pray for with respect to a small number of requests.

The first concern was a girl I shall call Diane. Diane was brought up on the wrong side of the tracks. She had no idea who her father was. Until her conversion at nursing school, she was coarse, crude – and frightened. Becoming a Christian made all the difference: she blossomed and flourished. Then, with two years behind her as a professional nurse, she was struck down with an acute kind of leukaemia. The prognosis was death within six weeks to two months.

Diane wrote me from her hospital bed 120 miles away, and her letter overflowed with bitterness, fear, self-pity, anger. What, then, should we pray for her? Should we pray, 'Lord, bless Diane'? Sometimes that is the only prayer we can honestly pray; we don't know enough to pray more. Or should we pray, 'Lord, take Diane home'? Or, 'Lord, heal her!'? We had no doubts the Lord *could* heal her; but neither of us was convinced that God was going to heal her. Whatever faith is, it is not churning up your stomach to believe something will happen that your head says will not happen.

What to pray for? My colleague and I prayed for wisdom and turned to Scripture. We were both quite sure that Diane was a Christian; and we remembered the many promises to the effect that God will keep his own people. So we prayed that God would honour his Word and fulfil his promises in Diane's case. We prayed this *in Jesus' name*, with perfect faith, because we knew this was in accord with his pledged Word.

That was Monday night. Thursday I received a letter from Diane, written on Tuesday. She said she had awakened with joy, and found herself singing hymns. She had come to find rest, deep rest, in the Lord's perfect will; and she was looking forward to going home to be with him, if that was what he wanted. Diane's letter suffused a deep love for and a resting faith in the Lord Jesus.

She died a few weeks later, but not before she exercised a remarkable influence in that hospital where she worked, suffered and died.

The next Monday evening prayer time took on deeper significance than any prayer I had ever known before. For a start, we were full of thanksgiving. Moreover, we had prayed for eight things the week before, and three were answered as dramatically as the one I have detailed. Three others were long-range requests; and the last two we changed as we gathered more light from Scripture on the questions with which we were dealing.

I almost hesitate to tell this story of the weekly prayer sessions. It is dramatic, and my times of prayer have not always been dramatic. Nor is it right to leave the impression that this is the only legitimate approach to intercession, still less that I am some spiritual giant who has mastered the art of prayer. I am a pilgrim, not a particularly faithful one, who still struggles with these basic questions. But of this I am sure: the intimacy between the believer and Jesus Christ is an intimacy whose fruit is the result of prayer under Christ's Lordship. What is necessary, then, is an increasing knowledge of the Scriptures so that we may learn how to pray with confidence in Jesus' name.

We also learn from this verse something of the nature of the 'fruit' in this chapter. Some want it to be measured in terms of lives brought to Christ in evangelism; others prefer to think of the 'fruit of the Spirit' in Galatians 5. But if I understand the passage correctly, both interpretations are too narrow. The fruit is everything done in conformity to the will of Jesus Christ, not least praying and loving. Jesus does not become more specific than that; he does not need to. Loving one another because of Jesus is Christian fruit; praying in Jesus' name, 'according to his will', as 1 John 5 puts it, is Christian fruit. Everything in our lives that brings glory to the Father (15:8) is Christian fruit. And the intimacy we enjoy with Jesus Christ, like the union of the branch with the vine, issues in such fruitfulness.

God grant us large and clear vision of these truths, and profound experience of them.

6 (John 15:17 – 16:4)

Counting the Cost

'This is my command: Love each other.

'If the world hates you, keep in mind that it hated me first. If you belonged to the world, it would love you as its own. As it is, you do not belong to the world, but I have chosen you out of the world. That is why the world hates you. Remember the words I spoke to you: "No servant is greater than his master." If they persecuted me, they will persecute you also. If they obeyed my teaching, they will obey yours also. They will treat you this way because of my name, for they do not know the One who sent me. If I had not come and spoken to them, they would not be guilty of sin. Now, however, they have no excuse for their sin. He who hates me hates my Father as well. If I had not done among them what no-one else did, they would not be guilty of sin. But now they have seen these miracles, and yet they have hated both me and my Father. But this is to fulfil what is written in their Law: "They hated me without reason."

'When the Counsellor comes, whom I will send to you from the Father, the Spirit of truth who goes out from the Father, he will testify about me; but you also

must test-ify, for you have been with me from the
beginning.

'All this I have told you so that you will not go astray.
They will put you out of the synagogue; in fact, a time is
coming when anyone who kills you will think he is offering a service to God. They will do such things because
they have not known the Father or me. I have told you
this, so that when the time comes you will remember
that I warned you. I did not tell you this at first because
I was with you.'

The verses at the beginning of John 15, discussed in chapter 5 of this book, present something of the glories of
being a Christian: intimacy with Jesus Christ, spiritual
fruitfulness, loving association with other 'branches',
productive prayer. These are causes for the greatest joy
and hope.

But are there no painful aspects to being a Christian?
Is all happiness and light, though Christ himself was a
man of sorrows who walked through the valley of the
shadow of death? Do we participate only in his joy, but
not in his tears? Does he alone bear the cross?

Even to ask such questions is to show that much
modern evangelicalism borders on the frivolous. We are
so often taught to think that the Christian way brings
blessings without bufferings, triumphs without trials,
witness without weariness. We are encouraged to
believe that Christians exude overcoming joy, and rarely
face discouraging defeat; that they live in a realm of constant excitement, and never wrestle with boredom; that
they love and are loved, and need not confront persecution, ostracism, hate, rejection; that they are self-confi-
dent and ebullient, and never taste terror, loneliness,
doubt; that they are fulfilled and satisfied, but not as a
result of self-denial and daily death. It is not so much

that the promises are false, that they have no substance, as that they distort truth by promising a crown without a cross. We too easily want the fruitfulness of a well-kept vine-branch, but think little about the disciplined pruning performed by the divine 'gardener'.

Jesus does not gloss over the difficult bits. If salvation comes to the house of Zacchaeus, it brings large principles of restitution (Luke 19:1–10). If Jesus tells the wonderful parable of the prodigal son and emphasizes the Father's forbearance and forgiveness (Luke 15:11–32), he also tells parables designed to encourage would-be disciples to count the cost (Luke 14:25-35). Towards the end of Luke 9, three vignettes are presented of people who volunteer to follow Jesus enthusiastically. Such people today might well find themselves quickly baptized, enrolled and witnessing, caught up in evangelical efficiency. In these three instances, however, Jesus puts up careful barriers designed to test the level of the proffered commitment:

> As they were walking along the road, a man said to him, 'I will follow you wherever you go.'
>
> Jesus replied, 'Foxes have holes and birds of the air have nests, but the Son of Man has no place to lay his head.'
>
> He said to another man, 'Follow me.'
>
> But the man replied, 'Lord, first let me go and bury my father.'
>
> Jesus said to him, 'Let the dead bury their own dead, but you go and proclaim the kingdom of God.'
>
> Still another said, 'I will follow you, Lord; but first let me go back and say good-bye to my family.'
>
> Jesus replied, 'No-one who puts his hand to the plough and looks back is fit for service in the kingdom of God.' (Luke 9:57–62)

Something similar takes place in John 15:17 – 16:4.
Having already expounded something of the glories of
being a disciple, Jesus now carefully enunciates something of the cost. Christians will face not only the pressures common to all mankind this side of the fall, but
will also face special difficulties that are part and parcel
of being a Christian. These difficulties arise from the fact
that opposition from the worldly-minded is inevitable,
that alignment with Jesus must inevitably evoke the
same hatred that was directed towards Jesus.

Three special difficulties must be expected by every
generation of Christians:

Christians must expect to meet the hatred of the world (15:17–25)

This prospect is best set forth under a number of important principles.

*1. The hatred of the world stands in marked contrast to the
love among God's people.* 'This is my command,' Jesus
says: 'Love each other. If the world hates you, keep in
mind that it hated me first' (15:17–18). In some ways,
verse 17 is transitional; but the harsh juxtaposition of
verses 17 and 18 is no accident. It brings out the sharp
contrast between the nature of the 'world' (in John's use
of the term) and the nature of the Christian community.
It is natural for the world to hate; it is natural for
Christians to love. Indeed, the words, 'If the world hates
you' do not bring the world's hatred into doubt; for
the expression means, 'If the world hates you – and it
does – . . .'

This principle cuts several different ways. John's
Gospel presupposes that Christians will in fact love one

another; and this theme becomes so important in John's first epistle that love becomes one of three tests which verify the validity of professing Christianity (1 John 3:10–24; 4:7–21; the other two tests are moral obedience to Christ's commands, and belief in right doctrines crucial to Christianity; and the three tests are interrelated). Christians must therefore be aware of creeping bitterness, resentment, or hatred in the body, and expunge it with love as quickly as possible. The so-called Christian group which reflects no love and concern at all is simply not Christian, regardless of the orthodoxy of its beliefs.

On the other hand, this passage does not deny that the world can show any love at all. Pagan parents may love their pagan infants; unbelieving men and women fall in love. But it is natural for the world to hate. The 'world' is made up of people who have never acknowledged the supremacy of Christ nor known the love of God. By definition, these people are absorbed either with themselves or with their self-created gods. It is impossible for them to love God or to love his people unless and until they set aside their false values, come to terms with the truth, and see their own position and role in the light of God's sovereignty and grace.

Nowhere is the world's hatred more clearly set forth than in those many people who judge themselves to be 'liberal' but who are most illiberal when it comes to Christian absolutes. They demonstrate their forbearance and large-hearted goodness when they confront diverse opinions, varied lifestyles and even idiotic practices. But if some Christian claims that Christianity is exclusive (as Jesus insisted), or that moral absolutes exist because they are grounded in the character of God (as the Bible teaches), or that there is a hell to be shunned as well as a heaven to be gained, the most intemperate language is used to excoriate the poor fool. The world hates.

2. The world hates because the world and the church are mutually exclusive; and the world resents any lack of conformity to itself. 'If you belonged to the world, it would love you as its own. As it is, you do not belong to the world, but I have chosen you out of the world. That is why the world hates you' (15:19).

The point is akin to that made by James, the half-brother of our Lord: 'You adulterous people, don't you know that friendship with the world is hatred towards God? Anyone who chooses to be a friend of the world becomes an enemy of God' (Jam. 4:4). Presupposed is the fact that the Christian, by definition, stands under the Lordship of Jesus Christ; and the world, by definition, does not stand under that Lordship. The church and the world are therefore heading in different directions, operating under different orders and cherishing distinct allegiances. This fundamental opposition between the world and the church is revealed in the strongest language when John says, 'You, dear children, are from God . . . They are from the world and therefore speak from the viewpoint of the world, and the world listens to them. We are from God, and whoever knows God listens to us; but whoever is not from God does not listen to us' (1 John 4:4–6). This is not a narrow-minded 'I'm-right-and-you're-wrong' attitude, a defensive exclusivism both haughty and opinionated which cannot discuss anything with anyone and which is not open to correction. Rather, it is the recognition that if God has truly revealed himself in Jesus Christ, then anything which cannot be reconciled with that truth or which wilfully refuses to listen to that truth is necessarily in error. It is a simple point of logic; but that simple point stands at the basis of an absolute polarity between the genuine believer and the worldly man.

That the church and the world are mutually exclusive does not by itself constitute a sufficient reason for the world's hatred. That hatred stems from the resentment the world exhibits towards all who refuse to conform to its perspectives. This does not mean that there is only one kind of 'world'. There is only one truth; but there are many kinds of error. In this sense there are many 'worlds'; or, better, the world wears many ugly faces. A system like Nazism is essentially anti-God; and, like Communism at the other end of the political spectrum, it has attempted to enforce conformity to its values and norms by coercive violence. The Nazi and the Communist hate each other; but both hate the genuine believer, and seek to make him conform to something essentially anti-Christian.

One need not turn to totalitarian governments to discover examples of 'worldliness' that resent the Christians' peculiar identity. Raw secularism, greedy materialism, unmoral special-interest groups seeking privilege or 'alternative lifestyles' which are biblically indefensible, all with one accord resent the Christian who stands up and lovingly insists, 'Thus says the Lord.' In the West, our temptations to conform stem less from the fear of brute force than from the fear of ostracism or disdain: contrast the temptations of brothers and sisters in, say, Russia. But our temptations are for that very reason more treacherous, more insidious, more dangerous. We do not always recognize that we are being duped.

Success and wealth, for example, are sometimes presented as the inevitable result of victorious Christian living; and the careless believer, deceived by this heresy, soon cannot distinguish his pursuit of God from his pursuit of things. Hedonism parades itself in the guise of fulfilment, licence in the guise of liberty, schism in the guise of orthodoxy, action in the guise of unction. Pressures increase until the believer feels guilty that he does not belong to some special 'in' group; and the 'in' group insists on such conformity that those outside are vilified to some degree. In some areas of North America, believing young people face enormous peer pressure because they separate themselves from drugs and pre-marital sex: purity is the exception, not the rule, and the Christian begins to feel the world's resentment. The cry is always the same: Conform! Conform!

During the period when the Anabaptists frequently found themselves persecuted by Protestants and Catholics alike, and bringing up their families while on the run, they faced the difficult decision of when to bap-tize their children. They had abandoned infant baptism, and embraced the view that people should be baptized only when they came to a personal knowledge of Jesus Christ through faith, a personal knowledge character-ized by unqualified obedience. But when should they baptize their children? Should an Anabaptist child who, while still very young, seemed to exercise saving faith in Jesus Christ be baptized, or made to wait for a few years? The response of the Anabaptists may not please everyone; but at least it showed their sensitivity to the fundamental opposition between world and church. In the case of the young child who professed faith, they deferred baptism until he or she grew old enough not only to face the temptations of the world, to feel the lure of the pressure to conform, to sense the resentment towards all failure to conform – *but also to turn his back, self-consciously and spiritually, on all such temptations and the options they represented*. Young believers need to rec-ognize, now as then, that the world and the church are mutually exclusive, and that the world resents any lack of conformity to itself.

3. *The world hates us because it hated Jesus Christ.* 'If the world hates you,' Jesus says, 'keep in mind that it hated

me first' (15:18). But more than chronological priority is at stake: there is the broader question of our identity with Jesus' teaching and our submission to Jesus' Lordship. That is why Jesus goes on to say, 'Remember the words I spoke to you: "No servant is greater than his master." If they persecuted me, they will persecute you also. If they obeyed my teaching, they will obey yours also' (15:20).

The heart of this verse is the clause in which Jesus quotes his own words: 'No servant is greater than his master.' In John's Gospel, these words are first uttered in 13:16 in the context of the foot-washing episode. There, Jesus sets an example for his disciples: he, the master, has accepted the despised task of foot-washing; and because 'no servant is greater than his master', the disciples ought to adopt a very humble and helpful stance towards one another.

Now Jesus refers to the same words in a different context. If no servant is above his master, and the master himself suffers the opprobrium of the world, it follows that the servants must expect similar persecution. Indeed, should any servant question by what principle he should be made to suffer, the answer is the same: No servant is greater than his master. If any would-be servant of Jesus thinks it his right to avoid opposition and even persecution, he is profoundly lacking in humility. He fails to see his proper place in relation to the Master. Jesus says as much elsewhere: 'A student is not above his teacher, nor a servant above his master. It is enough for the student to be like his teacher, and the servant like his master. If the head of the house has been called Beelzebub, how much more the members of his household!' (Matt. 10:24–25).

To belong to Christ is to invite some of the hatred directed at Christ. In one sense, of course, that is profoundly reassuring. We must not think the world's animosity is aimed at us personally, on the basis of what we are of ourselves. Far from it: it is our identification with Christ which arouses opposition. Should we be called upon to suffer, this perspective will enable us to follow the example of the apostles who, when they were flogged and abused, rejoiced 'because they had been counted worthy of suffering disgrace for the Name' (Acts 5:41). Conversely, when we are well received in Jesus' name, when congregations praise us and Christian brothers and sisters extend lavish, loving approval, it is helpful to remember that, just as we are persecuted for Jesus' sake, so also are we loved for Jesus' sake. Christians are neither hated nor loved, neither rejected nor believed, on their own account, but on account of Jesus Christ.

But why should people hate Jesus? What harm has he done? In the days of his flesh he robbed no banks, raped no-one, murdered no-one, slandered no-one. He was known for his healing power, his words of truth, his unflagging integrity, and for the rich texture of his love. Why, then, should people hate Jesus, and his disciples after him? The next two principles answer this question:

4. *The world hates because its sin is exposed.* 'If I had not come and spoken to them, they would not be guilty of sin. Now, however, they have no excuse for their sin . . . If I had not done among them what no-one else did, they would not be guilty of sin. But now they have seen these miracles, and yet they have hated both me and my Father' (15:22,24).

Jesus is not by these verses saying that men would have been totally innocent if he had not come and spoken to them and performed his miracles. This is made clear by several factors: The 'world' to which Jesus comes in the Gospel of John is already a sinful and rebellious world before he arrives on the scene. For example, he is sent as the Lamb of God to take away the world's sin (1:29). Note also that the formal antithesis in verse 22 is never completed. The text has two parts:

(1) If I had not come and spoken to them, they would not be guilty of sin.
(2) Now, however, they have no excuse for their sin.

Formally, however, a tight antithesis would require that (2) read: 'Now, however, they have become guilty of sin.' But this rigid antithesis, which would make Jesus the explicit cause of the world's sin, is avoided. Because Jesus has come, the world does not become sinful; rather, it is robbed of all excuse for its sin. This suggests the world was thoroughly sinful *before* Jesus came.

Close observation of the context suggests that the sin in view is specific. In the preceding verse, Jesus tells his disciples, 'They will treat you this way because of my name, *for they do not know the One who sent me*' (15:21). Then Jesus immediately adds, 'If I had not come and spoken to them, they would not be guilty of sin' (15:22). The sin they are guilty of is the sin of not knowing God even when God reveals himself most spectacularly and explicitly in Jesus Christ; for the world rejects this revelation of God, and the rejection turns to persecution and hatred.

Ever since the fall, the world has been sinning against God. But not until the coming of Jesus Christ, the perfect revelation of God, did the world ever sin against such light 'This is the verdict: Light has come into the world, but men loved darkness instead of light because their deeds were evil. Everyone who does evil hates the light, and will not come into the light for fear that his deeds will be exposed' (3:19–20). The disciples by themselves cannot arouse the world's ire, for they do not adequately challenge the world's evil; but Jesus is so pure that dirty men must either get cleaned up or else loathe his purity. So Jesus says to his disciples, 'The world cannot hate you, but it hates me because I testify that what it does is evil' (7:7).

So clear, so pure, so brilliant is the revelation of God in Jesus Christ that the world is robbed of all excuse when it confronts him. Its excuses never amounted to much; now they amount to nothing. Not only does Jesus expose sin; he is also sin's only remedy. What excuse and what hope can there be for those who turn away from such light as this? The world confronts Jesus, and either, by God's grace, turns from its sin (and thereby ceases to be the 'world' in John's sense), or else hates both Jesus and his Father (15:24).

In short, the world hates because its sin is exposed. It has always been so. Why did Cain murder Abel? 'Because his own actions were evil and his brother's were righteous' (1 John 3:12*b*). The problem is simply rendered more acute with the advent of purity as great as Christ's. To come to Jesus and confess him as Saviour and Lord requires contribution, a bended knee. One cannot come to Christ sensing no need, no unworthiness, no sin; one cannot come with head held high as a partner in the enterprise of salvation. It is impossible; for the light of the gospel in the Person of Jesus simultaneously illumines our grimy and corrupt hearts and points to him who alone makes all things clean and new. In that moment of self-revelation, either the grace of God takes hold and the sinner cries for mercy, for cleansing, for life; or else he loathes the light that has exposed the dirt. The latter is the reaction of the 'world'; and it is a principal ground of the world's hatred.

To a degree, Christians today evoke the same bifurcated reactions. We do not present ourselves, but Christ; yet as the light of Christ is mirrored through us to this dark world, exposing its venom and earning its implacable hatred, our association with Christ and our increasing conformity to him attracts the same hatred that Christ himself attracts. Paul understands this well; for he writes in a moving passage, 'But thanks be to God, who always leads us in triumphal procession in Christ and through us spreads everywhere the fragrance of the knowledge of him. For we are to God the aroma of Christ among those who are being saved and those who are perishing. To the one we are the smell of death; to the other, the fragrance of life. And who is equal to such a task?' (2 Cor. 2:14–16). The Christian's witness spreads the fragrance of Christ by his or her presence and words, by conduct and by testimony. But that sweet fragrance, while perceived by some to be the aroma of new life erupting in God's springtime, is perceived by others to be the stench of rotting corpses. Like Christ, Christians cannot but be divisive in this sense. It comes as a great relief to learn in the next chapter that the Counsellor, the Holy Spirit, helps us in this ministry of exposing the world's sin (16:8–11).

This principle has many important implications for comprehending the world's reaction to believers. The thing to note, as J.C. Ryle puts it, is obvious once stated: 'It is not the weaknesses and inconsistencies of Christians that the world hates, but their grace.' A Christian may be persecuted at work for refusing to cheat a customer. A Christian police officer in a Canadian force was not promoted for years because he quietly but firmly refused to participate in his commanding officer's addiction to alcohol. Only when a yet more senior officer heard of the problem was it overcome; and, to the Christian's credit, he was not the one who brought it to light. A Christian working in a warehouse, discovering that certain merchandise had been damaged after its arrival, refused to sign slips that said the goods had arrived in a defective condition. He was unceremoniously shunted to another department. The irony of such treatment is that the Christian's integrity is prized when it is in the company's favour, and despised when it stands in the way of profits or camaraderie.

Even the fact that Jesus has chosen the disciples out of the world (15:19) is enough to call forth the world's hatred. Christians are not some alien group, some collection of essentially superior beings. They are by nature themselves part and parcel of the world. Yet because of Jesus Christ they have left the world behind; and the world is not pleased. A cheater who stops cheating will not remain on intimate terms with other cheaters. A liar who stops lying will not be cherished by other liars. A raw secularist who abandons secularism for Christ cannot expect to win laurels from his secularist friends. To be chosen out of the world by Christ brings the opprobrium of the world; for the world cannot bear to have its sins exposed.

5. The world hates because it does not know the Father, nor recognize the revelation of the Father in the Son, 'They will treat you this way because of my name, *for they do not know the One who sent me* . . . He who hates me hates my Father as well. . . . But now they have seen these miracles, and yet they have hated both me and my Father . . . They will do such things because they have not known the Father or me (15:21,23,24b; 16:3).

When the text says that the world will persecute Jesus' disciples 'because of [Jesus'] name', it probably means no more than 'because of Jesus' or 'for Jesus' sake'. The real *ground* of the world's malicious opposition lies in its ignorance of both the Father and the Son.

In certain circumstances, the plea of ignorance is an adequate defence. I cannot be blamed because I am ignorant of Swahili (unless for some reason I am supposed to be learning it). I cannot be blamed because I am ignorant of what lies physically beyond the known universe, or because I enjoy no personal knowledge of Her Majesty Queen Elizabeth II. In other words, some kinds of ignorance do eliminate all suggestion of culpability. But other ignorance provides no excuse. As a driver I am responsible for knowing the speed limit that applies to the stretch of road over which I am driving. If for any reason I fail to read the posted limits, my plea of ignorance will count very little when the police officer tells me I am breaking the law. Indeed, not only is ignorance no excuse in such a situation, but my ignorance is itself culpable; for I am supposed to know what the limit is, and my ignorance attests my carelessness or inattention.

Human beings are supposed to know God. We were made in his image, and enough of his nature and character has been stamped on our conscience that we are eternally without excuse. I ought to know God, not merely some facts about him; and if I do not, my ignorance of him is already a sign of my rebellion against him, of my pursuit of other gods or of myself. Such ignorance is culpable.

For those who have access to the Scriptures, there is an additional reason why ignorance of God and of his revelation in Jesus Christ is guilty ignorance. It is this: the Scriptures long before Jesus foretell the coming of a 'prophet' whose words men are morally bound to heed. For instance, God declares to Moses, 'I will raise up for them a prophet like you from among their brothers; I will put my words in his mouth, and he will tell them everything I command him. *If anyone does not listen to my words that the prophet speaks in my name, I myself will call him to account'* (Deut. 18:18–19). With a warning such as that, the plea of ignorance is damning rather than exonerating.

Elsewhere, the fourth Gospel teaches that if a person truly knows Jesus Christ, that person knows the Father also (8:19); and such knowledge is the essence of eternal life (17:3). This way of phrasing it – that to know Jesus is to know God – presupposes that Jesus has come in history, and has become 'known' by certain people. Jesus mediates the knowledge of God. But the relationship between Jesus and his Father can be looked at another way. If people knew the Father *before* Jesus came in history, then they would recognize Jesus upon his arrival. Failure to know Jesus, therefore, testifies to ignorance of God before Jesus' arrival. But once the bright light of the revelation of God in Jesus Christ has taken place in history, it becomes better to phrase things the first way: if a person does not know Jesus, he cannot know the Father.

Thus, it is the arrival of Jesus Christ *in history* which changes the focus. Men could know God in Old Testament times under the covenantal stipulations laid down by God. Some did know him; and they constituted a faithful remnant who, by knowing God according to the light already revealed, were primed to know Christ. Those who did not know God and the perfection of his character and ways could only hate Christ; and, learning to hate Christ, they soon came to hate Christians. Their hatred and their opposition constituted bleak evidence that they had never known God. Once Christ had come *in history*, this Christ who is the ultimate revelation of God to a fallen world, then hatred directed towards Christ counted more and more as evidence that the world was cutting itself off from the one way to know God.

Whatever the order, Christians insist that, from the time of the revelation of Jesus Christ, to love Jesus is to love God, and to love God is to love Jesus. Conversely, not to know God is not to know Jesus, and not to know Jesus is not to know God. To know them is to possess eternal life (17:3); not to know them is to walk in eternal death, to love the shadows and the dark places where light is unwelcome and resented. To be ignorant of God is morally reprehensible, for that ignorance testifies to a moral alignment with evil, self-love and darkness. For this reason, ignorance of God often erupts in an ugly malice which persecutes Jesus and his followers (15:20–21), even to the point of crude violence (16:2–3).

6. *The world hates for no good reason; yet even this unreasonable hatred falls within the purview of the sovereignty of God.* Jesus speaks of the world's hatred in these terms: 'But this is to fulfil what is written in their Law: "They hated me without reason"' (15:25). (The word *Law* was often used to refer to the entire Bible of the Jews, not just the Pentateuch.) The passage cited is either Psalm 35:19 or Psalm 69:4. The latter is marginally more probable, because Psalm 69 was widely regarded as Messianic.

Jesus is here reported as taking a firm poke at the Jews: this book is *their* law (cf. also 10:34). It is *their* law, not because they invented it, but because they so jealously guard it even while failing to understand it. *Their* law condemned causeless hatred; *their* law predicted such groundless hatred against the Messiah. Yet, here they are, hating mightily – and without excuse. By the dictates of *their* own law, they stand self-condemned.

Why hate Jesus? One can *understand* why people hate Jesus, inasmuch as one can understand that sin does not want to be exposed and resents the searing brilliance of the light of truth and purity and love. But such factors betray the sad condition of the world; they do not provide any reason in Jesus himself for evoking such hatred. There may be things in Stalin or in Hitler which understandably call forth opposition and hatred; but what is there in Jesus? He went about doing good. As is usually the case, the judgments we make and the opinions we form say as much about us as they do about objects or persons being considered. From this perspective, hatred directed towards Jesus is utterly unreasonable.

The way Jesus cites this passage from the Psalms brings to light another truth: even the world's unreasonable hatred falls within the purview of the sovereignty of God. Jesus insists that all the animosity directed against him fulfils Scripture. In exactly the same way, Herod and Pontius Pilate conspired wickedly against Jesus, and succeeded in crucifying him; but they actually accomplished only what God had decided beforehand should happen (Acts 4:27–28; 2:23). The world's hatred against Jesus and his followers is not something unforeseen, something unexpected, which takes Jesus by surprise. On the contrary: it is the fulfilment of God's holy Word.

This can only be a source of encouragement to persecuted believers. The opposition we may endure aligns us with Jesus; and more, far from being a sign that things are almost out of control and that God's cause has only the most precarious foothold, it is the proof that God's salvation is transforming people, the evidence that his Word is being fulfilled. Even the world's unreasonable hatred cannot escape God's sovereignty. This is the triumphant assurance of believers who have come to grips with the first fundamental expectation: Christians must expect the hatred of the world. God has said it would come.

Christians must expect to serve as witnesses in this hating world, joining with the Counsellor in this work (15:26–27)

Jesus now goes on to say, 'When the Counsellor comes, whom I will send to you from the Father, the Spirit of truth who goes out from the Father, he will testify about me; but you also must testify, for you have been with me from the beginning' (15:26–27).

Christians must not think that Jesus Christ has left them in this world for no other purpose than to endure hatred. For the first disciples, the problem was particularly acute: why was Jesus leaving them behind? The text now insists that the coming Counsellor, the promised Spirit of truth, will testify to the world concerning Jesus; *and the disciples will join in that witness*. That is the reason why they are being left behind.

Those first Christians bore a special witness, in that they had been with Jesus 'from the beginning' of his ministry (15:27; cf. Acts 1:22; 10:37). Yet the commission to witness is not given to apostles only: to confess *with one's mouth* 'Jesus is Lord' is an integral part of being a Christian (Rom. 10:9). Today we who are Christians bear a similar responsibility to bear witness to Jesus in a world often characterized by hatred towards Jesus. We must expect to serve as witnesses in this world.

The prospect is not as bleak as might at first be thought. Just as Jesus during his ministry bore primary responsibility, and the disciples played a secondary role, so now the Holy Spirit bears primary responsibility, and, secondarily, we also must testify (15:27). To view our witness in such light tends to transform a responsibility into a privilege.

The work of the Counsellor in the world is discussed at greater length in 16:5–15 (chapter 7 in this book). For now it is necessary to point out only that the Holy Spirit may perform his work through the disciples. The witness of the Holy Spirit may be separable from the witness of the church; but usually the witness of the church and that of the Holy Spirit are inseparable.

The early church remembered such teaching as this, and cherished it. It is delightful to discover Peter and the other apostles standing up to the Sanhedrin and defending the resurrection of Jesus in these terms: 'We are witnesses of these things *and so is the Holy Spirit*, whom God has given to those who obey him' (Acts 5:32). They were conscious that they were not alone in their witness. The opponents of Stephen discovered 'they could not stand up against his wisdom *or the Spirit by which he spoke* (Acts 6:10). In times of sharp persecution, the church has always remembered Jesus' instruction: 'But when they arrest you, do not worry about what to say or how to say it. At that time you will be given what to say, for it will not be you speaking, *but the Spirit of your Father speaking through you*' (Matt. 10:19–20).

The wonder of these passages can be appreciated only by Christians who have witnessed under adverse circumstances of active opposition, and who have been conscious of the Holy Spirit's quiet work. How he accomplishes his work is not easy to analyse, and most of our formulations are no doubt reductionistic. He purifies the believers, grants them holy boldness, teaches them meekness, calls to their mind truth that is appropriate. He incites to prayer, opens our eyes to need, and increases our desire to do the will of God. At the same time he works in the hearts and minds of those who hear the witness, bringing them conviction of sin, opening their eyes, planting the Word and softening hard hearts. Christians who begin to glimpse the privilege of witness, who truly expect to serve as witnesses in this hating world but who recognize that they must lean on the Spirit of God throughout the endeavour, sing and pray with fervour:

> O Breath of Life, come sweeping through us,
>   Revive Thy Church with life and power;
> O Breath of Life, come, cleanse, renew us,
>   And fit Thy Church to meet this hour.

> O Wind of God, come bend us, break us,
>   Till humbly we confess our need;
> Then in Thy tenderness remake us,
>   Revive, restore; for this we plead.

> O Breath of Love, come breathe within us,
>   Renewing thought and will and heart:
> Come, Love of Christ, afresh to win us,
>   Revive Thy Church in every part.

> Revive, us, Lord! Is zeal abating
>   While harvest fields are vast and white?
> Revive us, Lord, the world is waiting,
>   Equip Thy Church to spread the light.
>
> *Bessie Porter Head (1850–1936)*

Christians must expect some bouts of severe persecution (16:1–4)

After insisting that Christians must expect to bear witness in a world characterized by hatred, Jesus presses on towards a still darker picture: sometimes crude and cruel violence will be directed at his followers. Not for them the cowardly silence of the Jewish leaders who would not confess their faith in Jesus 'for fear they

would be put out of the synagogue' (12:42). Such com-
promisers love praise from men more than praise from
God (12:43). True believers bear witness; but such witness often faces outbreaks of violent repression.

Three simple points are made. First, terrible persecution is inevitable (16:2). Important reading for every
Christian who wants to place this aspect of his heritage
in perspective is Foxe's *Book of Martyrs*. There we learn
the well-documented stories of believers burnt at the
stake, of Christians whose knee-caps were smashed,
whose children were drowned, whose joints were sys-
tematically and excruciatingly dislocated, whose testi-
cles were crushed – not because they were evil people,
but solely because they belonged to Christ. They join the
list of faith-heroes of whom the world is not worthy
(Heb. 11:35–38).

Two opposite errors confront us when we learn such
things. The first is to think that in some periods *all*
Christians of some locale faced intense suffering. Only
very rarely has this been the case. Christian leaders are
persecuted, along with a random sample of others; and
no doubt many of the rest live in fear they will face the
same end. Rarely, however, does an entire church face
physical violence. The second possible error is to suppose that the age of martyrdom has just about ceased.
Such a judgment is painfully ill-informed. We need not
think only of memorable stories, like the spearing of the
five missionaries by the Aucas in Ecuador, but also of the
believers trapped in the *Gulag* who are imprisoned and
killed for their faith. We think of men such as Dietrich
Bonhoeffer and those who died for similar beliefs under
the Nazis; and we remember the countless millions who
died under Mao's purges (conservative estimates are
twelve million), at least some of these simply because
they were Christians. As I write, it is estimated that an

average of three pastors are being put to death each week in Ethiopia. Most missiologists estimate that there have been more Christian martyrs in the twentieth century than in all of the previous centuries of the Christian era combined. Unless the Lord grants renewal and reformation, it is difficult to think of any reason why we who live in the Western world will escape such evils indefinitely.

The second point to observe is that some of the worst persecutions will be done in the name of God, even though God remains unknown to the persecutors. 'A time is coming', Jesus warns, 'when anyone who kills you will think he is offering a service to God. They will do such things because they have not known the Father or me' (16:2*b*–3). This is hard to believe; but a sermon was preached when Archbishop Cranmer was burnt, and the ghastly horrors of the Inquisition were performed by men claiming to defend the truth of God.

But the third and most important point is that Jesus tells his disciples these things not to frighten them off, but to enable them to stand. 'All this I have told you so that you will not go astray' (16:1), Jesus says. If persecution had come on them without warning, perhaps it would have prompted defection and apostasy. Because Jesus has carefully prepared his church, however, it usually transpires that 'the blood of the martyrs is the seed of the church'. 'I have told you this,' Jesus adds, 'so that when the time comes you will remember that I warned you. I did not tell you this at first because I was with you' (16:4). As long as Jesus was physically present, he did not need to stress this prospect; for not only was he present to offer comfort, but his very presence attracted almost all of the opposition away from the disciples towards himself. Now, he says, he is leaving; and he not only prepares his followers for what lies ahead, but gets them ready to serve as the front-line target once he himself is no longer present to draw the hottest fire.

It is difficult for some to believe that a cause is truly God's unless it is constantly on the ascendancy. When a movement is relatively weak, few in numbers, and without any of the clout a pagan or secular world appreciates, it is hard for some to accept that it is of God. But we must remember that this is the path the Lord Jesus himself travelled.

The way of the cross is the Saviour's way. Those who claim all the blessings of the new heaven and the new earth in the present time-frame have not come to grips with New Testament eschatology. True, the age to come has dawned, and the Holy Spirit himself is the down payment of future bliss; but it does not follow that all material blessings, prosperity, and freedom from opposition are rightfully ours now. Even John, who of the New Testament writers is most inclined to focus attention on the already-inaugurated features of the age to come, makes it clear that the Christian can in this age expect hatred, persecution, and even violence.

Perhaps this chapter, taken by itself, might prove depressing to some. It is helpful to remember that the biblical passage being expounded, John 15:17 – 16:4, does not stand in isolation. It is the counterpoint to intimacy with Jesus Christ and rich fruit-bearing in the spiritual life. To know Jesus is to have eternal life; and this is worth everything. In ultimate terms, the acclaim of the world is worth nothing. That is why the dark brush-strokes of this passage, 15:17 – 16:4, far from fostering gloom and defeat, engender instead holy courage and spiritual resolve.

Meditation on these verses forges men and women of God with vision and a stamina whose roots reach into eternity. It calls forth a William Tyndale, who while constantly fleeing his persecutors worked at the translation of the Bible into English. Through betrayal, disappointment and fear, he struggled on until he was captured and burnt at the stake. His dying cry revealed his eternal perspective: 'Lord, open the King of England's eyes!'

In a similar vein, William Borden prepared for missionary service in the Muslim world. Born to wealth, he poured his money and his example into missions. After the best of training at Yale University and Princeton Seminary, he arrived in Egypt to work with Samuel Zwemer. Almost immediately he contracted a terminal case of cerebral meningitis. His dying testimony did not falter: 'No reserve; no retreat; no regrets.'

C.T. Studd, born to privilege, gifted athletically, and trained at Eton and Cambridge, turned his back on wealth and served Christ for decades against unimaginable odds, first in China and then in Africa. He penned the words:

Some want to live within the sound
  of church or chapel bell;
I want in build a rescue shop
  within yards of hell.

This is the passion we need: a passion that looks at the mountainous difficulties and exults that we are on the winning side. By all means, let us face the worst: Christ has told us these things so we shall not go astray.

Soldiers of Christ, arise,
  And put your armour on;
Strong in the strength which God supplies
  Through His eternal Son;

Strong in the Lord of hosts,
  And in His mighty power;

Who in the strength of Jesus trusts
  Is more than conqueror.

From strength to strength go on;
  Wrestle, and fight, and pray;
Tread all the powers of darkness down,
  And win the well-fought day:

That, having all things done,
  And all your conflicts past,
Ye may o'ercome, through Christ alone,
  And stand complete at last.

Charles Wesley (1707–88)

Two Special Ministries of the Spirit

'Now I am going to him who sent me, yet none of you asks me, "Where are you going?" Because I have said these things, you are filled with grief. But I tell you the truth: It is for your good that I am going away. Unless I go away, the Counsellor will not come to you; but if I go, I will send him to you. When he comes, he will convict the world of guilt in regard to sin and righteousness and judgment: in regard to sin, because men do not believe in me; in regard to righteousness, because I am going to the Father, where you can see me no longer, and in regard to judgment, because the prince of this world now stands condemned.

'I have much more to say to you, more than you can now bear. But when he, the Spirit of truth, comes, he will guide you into all truth. He will not speak on his own; he will speak only what he hears, and he will tell you what is yet to come. He will bring glory to me by taking from what is mine and making it known to you. All that belongs to the Father is mine. That is why I said the Spirit will take from what is mine and make it known to you.'

Jesus now returns to the ministry of the Holy Spirit, the promised Counsellor.

What is the connection between 16:5–15 and the rest of the Farewell Discourse? Superficially, there is a formal connection between 16:4 and 16:5. The former finds Jesus explaining why he has been outlining the dangers of coming persecution; and he sums up by saying, rather proleptically, 'I did not tell you this at first because I was with you.' John 16:5 reminds us afresh of Jesus' impending departure: 'Now I am going to him who sent me.'

In terms of subject-matter, the connection between 16:5–15 and the rest of the Farewell Discourse runs at a deeper level. Three themes already treated are again brought up, two of them for detailed comment. The first, and least significant, is the disciples' grief at Jesus' departure. The second is the role of the Holy Spirit in the world. This is of special importance in view of the emphases just laid down: the followers of Jesus must expect to serve as witnesses in a world that easily hates them and sometimes persecutes them. Jesus has already assured his disciples that the Counsellor will participate in that witness; and here he explains in a rich but compressed statement just what the Counsellor will do.

The third theme introduces a pause in the flow of the Discourse. Aware that his disciples cannot take in any more until after the cross, Jesus opts to promise them more information and explanation when they are better able to handle it. This instruction will come by the ministry of the Counsellor, the Spirit of truth; and his role in this regard is explored a little further.

Jesus' opening remark, on the face of it, is rather strange: 'Now I am going to him who sent me, yet none of you asks me, "Where are you going?"' (16:5). Has he so soon forgotten that this very question was asked by

Simon Peter and implied by Thomas a little earlier in the evening (13:36; 14:5)?

Attempts to circumnavigate this difficulty are not very convincing. One commentator tries to resolve the problem by laying much stress on the present tense of the verb: 'yet none of you [now] *asks* me' rather than 'yet none of you [earlier] *asked* me'. This use of the present tense is, however, probably incidental. The fourth Gospel often uses verbs in the present for both past and future; and in any case it seems churlish on Jesus' part if he is rebuking his disciples for failing to ask afresh a question they have already twice posed that same evening. Such a rebuke would suggest that Jesus is grov-elling for pity in a way quite at odds with the flow of the Farewell Discourse.

Another commentator suggests Jesus is reproaching his men not because they are failing to inquire about his destination, but because in spite of knowing he is return-ing to his Father they cannot face the future without fear. The problem with this interpretation is that it flies in the face of what 16:5 explicitly says. Jesus rebukes his disci-ples for failing to ask 'Where are you going?', not for complaining about this fear.

Two considerations point the way out of the dilemma. First, although Peter's question was phrased in terms of Jesus' destination ('Where are you going?'), in fact it was concerned not with Jesus' destination but with his departure. In that sense Peter had not really asked the question his words seem to convey. An example makes this obvious. A father may assure his children on Friday that the next day they'll spend some time together in the park. Saturday dawns, and the phone rings to inform the father that some emergency has erupted in the machin-ery at work and requires his immediate presence. It will take at least twelve hours to make the needed repairs.

No sooner does the father attempt to explain the change of plans to his child than the child interrupts him with the plaintive, whining question, 'Aw, where are you going?' But, like Peter, the child is in fact less concerned with destination than with departure. The question regarding destination has not really been asked at all, formal appearances notwithstanding.

That brings us to the second consideration. The disciples of Jesus, Peter included, are still so self-absorbed that they are not really asking sympathetic questions about what Jesus is doing, where he is going, and why. As in 14:28–29, they are so concerned with their own problems, their feeling of abandonment, their sense of impending crisis and doom, that they do not really *listen*. They love themselves much and their Master little; and therefore they neither rejoice with him in his prospect of returning to the Father, nor mourn with him in his prospect of the cross. They grieve only for themselves; and, regardless of how they are phrased, their questions are concerned only with themselves. That is why Jesus immediately goes on to say, 'Because I have said these things, you are filled with grief' (16:6).

Christians today need to meditate long on this rebuke. Some branches of Christendom stress the believer's experience, the believer's privilege, the believer's blessings, the believer's faith, the believer's love, the believer's conduct. Evangelism is done solely in terms of what is in it for the contact, not in terms of God's honour and glory. Crass appeals are framed in terms of how much converts can receive if only they believe the right way or sacrifice appropriately. Testimonies reflect the convert's experiences of contrition, joy, grief, triumph, love. None of this is necessarily bad, even if it is often unbalanced; but where is the focus on Jesus Christ himself, except as the one who dutifully pays the bills? Of course true Christianity transforms the personality and can be richly described in the categories of personal experience: but who is more concerned to please Jesus and fulfil Jesus' desires than to please himself and fulfil his own desires?

Other branches of Christendom underline the importance of sacrifice and the need for service. They insist on Christian participation in struggles for justice, and judge deficient all Christian profession that does not make disciplined self-denial a fundamental, central and controlling motif. Of course it is true that biblical Christianity demands self-denial and thrusts believers out in sacrificial service and profound sympathy for the outcast; but is it not possible to become so enamoured with the trappings of self-discipline and so occupied with the urgencies of injustice that activity displaces adoration and personal sacrifice dethrones a personal Saviour?

Still others tremble at the doctrinal declension which threatens to ravage Christianity from the inside. They see defection from a high view of Scripture as an evil of mind-numbing proportions, and warn against the syncretism which is surreptitiously intruding itself into the flaccid flanks of evangelicalism. Defenders of the truth, they scent heresy in the earliest stages and are quick to pounce on it and expose it. Of course, true Christianity is indeed a religion of the Book, and it boasts certain non-negotiable doctrines and exclusive claims – the denial of which places one outside the camp; but is it not possible to be orthodox and much concerned about correct formulations of the truth, while all the time only minimally concerned to follow *Jesus himself* in a full-orbed and adoring manner?

The disciples in John 16 do not fall into precisely these errors of imbalance. Nevertheless their conduct has one thing in common with such deficient representations of

Christianity: something other than Jesus himself and all that he is and says receives primary attention. The other things in question may be worthy, good, and even necessary: who, after all, would demean personal experience, sacrificial service, or firm commitment to truth? Yet if these good and essential things displace the centrality of Jesus Christ in our worship, empathy and commitment, we come close to prostituting the good news of Jesus and following the disciples' sorry example.

Because the disciples have been self-absorbed, they have still not come to grips with the fact that Jesus' departure is for their own good. Jesus therefore repeats this point: 'I tell you the truth: It is for your good that I am going away. Unless I go away, the Counsellor will not come to you; but if I go, I will send him to you' (16:7). The Spirit could not be given until Jesus was glorified (7:39). Only after Jesus had died on the cross to atone for our sin, had risen from the grave to demonstrate his victory, and had ascended into heaven to receive all dominion, could the Holy Spirit be bequeathed on Jesus' disciples. In the New Testament, the Spirit is the down payment of eternal life, the foretaste of the eternal, unshielded presence of Deity, the one who incorporates us into the body of Christ, the one who regenerates us and indwells us: how could these blessings possibly come to us until the basis for them was established? And that basis is the triumph of Christ, his return to the Father via the cross and the grave.

It is beyond question, then, that it is for the disciples' good that Jesus 'goes away'. This is soon to be reflected in their own experience, even if at the moment they are unable to appreciate the fact. Contrast the conduct of the followers of Jesus on this black night with their conduct several months down the road. In a few short hours, their behaviour would be so despicable (even if understandable) that a believer called John Mark would describe it tersely in these words: 'Then everyone deserted him and fled' (Mark 14:50). Yet a few weeks later, once the Holy Spirit had been poured out on them, they faced open hostility with courageous joy and triumphant faith, prompting Luke to write, 'And they were all filled with the Holy Spirit and spoke the word of God boldly' (Acts 4:31). Even when they were flogged, they testified with joy (Acts 5:41). Jesus in John 16 does not exaggerate: it is for the disciples' good that he goes away.

But what will the Counsellor do when he comes? Jesus unpacks two of his ministries in some detail.

The Counsellor, the Holy Spirit, comes to the disciples in order to convict the world (16:8–11)

'When he comes,' Jesus says, 'he will convict the world of guilt in regard to sin and righteousness and judgment: in regard to sin, because men do not believe in me; in regard to righteousness, because I am going to the Father, where you can see me no longer; and in regard to judgment, because the prince of this world now stands condemned' (16:8–11).

Before turning to a close study of this passage, two preliminary reflections are worth sorting out. The first is that these verses, however they are interpreted, suggest (although they do not explicitly state) that, apart from this work of the Counsellor, fallen human beings cannot truly come to grips with sin and righteousness and judgment. Earlier we wondered just how a person who belongs to the 'world', the world which can neither perceive Jesus by the eye of faith nor obey him, could ever cease belonging to the world and become a follower of Jesus. A partial answer is advanced in these verses. Even though the world cannot accept the Spirit of truth (14:17), nevertheless the Spirit of truth comes to convict the world. This could well serve as a stepping-stone to conversion.

The second reflection is more obvious. On the interpretation of these verses which I shall adopt, the Counsellor now functions more as a prosecutor than as counsel for the defence. In one sense, of course, both 'counsel for the defence' and 'prosecutor' are inadequate metaphors for the Holy Spirit. As counsel for the defence, the Holy Spirit does indeed help the 'defendant' – the Christian who is barraged by guilt, by a sense of his unworthiness, and by the charges of the devil. But this Counsellor does not 'defend' believers against an external judge, for that is the work of the Lord Jesus himself, who intercedes before his Father on our behalf.

The ransom has been paid and the pardon secured by the death and resurrection of Christ: that is the ground of Jesus' intercessory role (cf. Heb. 9:25–28). But that is also the ground upon which Christians ought to experience personal freedom from guilt: their debt has already been paid. The Counsellor has the task of defending his 'client' against his own doubts and fears, and against his spiritual adversaries, rather than before a judge. This is not the normal function of a 'counsel for the defence'.

Similarly, as a prosecutor the Holy Spirit aims to convict the defendant, the person who belongs to the world; but 'convict' in this context does not mean 'secure a conviction before a judge', but rather 'drive home personal conviction in an individual's heart and mind'. The aim of the Spirit's work is not to produce a guilty verdict – that already stands (3:18,36) – but to bring the defendant to see the perilous condition in which he stands. That may prompt him to enter a plea for mercy; for only mercy will save him.

These four verses, John 16:8–11, have called forth a great deal of debate. The reason they are so difficult to interpret aright is partly because in the Greek they are terribly compressed, and partly because it seems very difficult to build a consistent interpretation of the three main elements in the passage. Moreover, some of the words used have a very broad semantic range; and different interpreters adopt different meanings for them. For instance, some people think that the verb rendered 'will convict' in the NIV (16:8) means just that; others think it means 'will convince' or 'will expose'. Some argue that the Counsellor comes to convince *the disciples* of the *world's* guilt – an interpretation which would mean the Holy Spirit here functions only with respect to the believers, not the world.

Even little, common words in the text are hard to pin down. There is one Greek word behind the NRV's 'in regard to', and it is often translated 'concerning'. But if we understand the text to say that the Counsellor will convict the world concerning sin, we run into trouble in the next lines; for what does it mean to say that the Counsellor convicts the world concerning *righteousness?* Even if we say that the Spirit convicts the world of *the world's* sin and of *Christ's* righteousness (as many suggest), we have unconsciously tampered with the meaning of the verb *convicts*.

Many of the factors on which a proper understanding of this text turns are complex and technical; and this is not the place to go into them. Nor would it be wise at this juncture to provide a comprehensive list of the various positions that various scholars have adopted. Interested readers can always consult the larger commentaries. I propose rather to enlarge upon the interpretation of this passage which in my judgment best explains the grammar of the text and conforms to the theology of the fourth Gospel as a whole. I have defended this view at a technical level elsewhere, and shall not repeat myself here.[7]

It may be helpful to begin with a translation I would be prepared to defend, set out in a schematic way, and then proceed to exposition.

> When he comes, he will convict the world
> > of its sin,
> > its righteousness,
> > and its judgment:
> its sin,
> > because they do not believe in me;
> its righteousness,
> > because I am going to the Father and you will no
> > > longer see me;
> and its judgment,
> > because the prince of the world stands judged.

The Counsellor, the Holy Spirit, will convict the world of its sin: that is, he will bring the world to self-conscious recognition of personal and collective guilt. The reason he will discharge this ministry is provided in 16:9: the Counsellor convicts the world of its sin because the people who constitute the world do not believe in Jesus. Because the people of the world do not believe in Jesus, they do not accept his teaching, believe his claims, or adopt his assessment of them. They do not turn to him for salvation; they do not even discern their need of him. Therefore the Holy Spirit comes and convicts them of their sin. If he did not do so, there is no way that any person who is part of the world could ever break free from the chains of the world and turn to Jesus. Jesus would simply not be an option, because he would not be believed. Apart from the work of the Counsellor, the world refuses to acknowledge its sin and turn to Jesus, precisely because the world does not believe Jesus. The Holy Spirit brings conviction of sin to this unbelieving world anyway.

The passage also teaches that the Holy Spirit will convict the world of its righteousness. It must be admitted that the possessive 'its' is not found in the text, which reads, simply, that the Holy Spirit will convict the world 'of righteousness'. The question is: Whose righteousness? If *Jesus'* righteousness is in view, then clearly the Counsellor does not convict the world of *Jesus'* righteousness in exactly the same way he convicts the world of *its own* sin. One would have to suppose that the Spirit convicts the world of its sin, but *convinces* the world of Jesus' righteousness (thus producing an unwarranted change in the verb); or perhaps that the Spirit convicts the world of its sin and also *convicts the world of its shortcomings* in the light of Jesus' righteousness (which introduces an unwarranted explanatory note into the text).[8]

Such difficulties are overcome if the Spirit is convicting the world of *its sin*, and also convicting the world of *its righteousness*. This approach preserves a graceful symmetry in the passage. The only question is whether the word *righteousness* can bear the weight it must then support: i.e., 'righteousness' must then be taken ironically to refer to what the world holds to be righteousness, even if God judges it to be unrighteousness. Can the word be legitimately understood in this ironic way?

The answer is surely affirmative. The fourth Gospel is much given to irony. Even John's most sacred of verbs, *to believe*, is sometimes used to refer to faith that is less than acceptable (e.g. 2:23–25). In other words, there is both good and bad belief; why not also both good and bad righteousness? Even in the Old Testament, 'righteousness' could be false and evil. In Isaiah 64:6, for

instance, we are told that the righteousness of the people
(in the Greek LXX, the same word is used as is found in
John 16) is like a menstruous cloth.

Moreover, although the word *righteousness* is found
only once in John's Gospel, considerable reproach is
thrown on the Jews for their self-righteousness – even
where the word is not used. The flow of the drama
makes the point most tellingly, without underscoring it
in a heavy-handed way. The temple, which is the very
centre of Jewish worship, is not only cleansed, but displaced by Jesus' body (2:13–22): that is, the true means of
righteousness focuses not on temple worship but on
Jesus' death. The Pharisees carefully observe the
Sabbath regulations, but show no delight that a man
thirty-eight years a paralytic has been healed (5:16).
There is much pious study of the Scriptures, but an utter
failure to grasp their true subject (5:39–40). The leaders,
even though they possess the law of Moses, go so far as
to attempt to kill Jesus (7:19); and some of them, while
secretly believing in Jesus, refuse to confess him,
because they are motivated by fear of excommunication
(they want to fit into human patterns of righteousness
rather than adopt God's perspective on the matter
[12:42–43]). Small wonder, then, that the Holy Spirit
must convict the world of *its righteousness*.

The idea of false, human righteousness is paralleled
by several passages in Paul. The Jews, Paul insists, 'did
not know the *righteousness* that comes from God and
sought to establish *their own*' (Rom. 10:3). In so doing,
they 'did not submit to God's righteousness'. If God
saved us, it is 'not because of *righteous things* we had
done, but because of his mercy' (Titus 3:5). Paul himself
in his pre-Christian days could claim a certain faultless
righteousness; but once he becomes a believer, all such
things which he formerly reckoned to his profit he now

dismisses as 'rubbish' and 'loss for the sake of Christ' (Phil. 3:6–9). 'I consider them rubbish,' he writes, 'that I may gain Christ and be found in him, *not having a right-eousness of my own that comes from the law*, but that which is through faith in Christ' (Phil. 3:8*b*–9).

The Holy Spirit continues this work today; and it is sorely needed. Men and women of the world do not ordinarily think of themselves as lost, as sinners. They think of themselves as essentially righteous. If the Lamb of God came to take away the sin of the world, then surely, they suppose, it must be somebody else's sin. If we are good citizens, helpful in the community, upright, and even scrupulously religious, is that not enough?

No; it is not enough. Even a man of such extraordinary credentials as Nicodemus (John 3) needed to be born again. And until a person satisfied with his own right-eousness perceives its inadequacy, its self-centredness, its shortcomings, its imperfections – in other words, until he is convicted of his righteousness in exactly the same way he is convicted of his sin – it is difficult to perceive how the gospel will be received as good news.

Jesus says that the Counsellor will convict the world of its righteousness 'because I am going to the Father, where you can see me no longer' (16:10). In the last chapter, we saw that one of Jesus' crucial functions during his earthly ministry was to expose the world's sin, to set the world's false righteousness over against his own matchless righteousness (see especially 15:22–24). But now Jesus is leaving this earthly setting: who will continue to show up the world's righteousness for what it really is, and drive home conviction of sin and false righteousness? The answer is provided by the text: the Holy Spirit will convict the world of its righteousness *because Jesus* is going to the Father. In this respect, the Counsellor takes over the ministry of Jesus.

Why, then, does verse 10 end with the words, 'where *you* can see me no longer'? Why this second-person pronoun, instead of third? Would it not be more coherent to think of the Holy Spirit convicting the world of its righteousness because Jesus is going away and *the world* (rather than the disciples) can no longer see him? That would certainly make eminently good sense; so we must ask why the disciples are introduced.

The answer turns on two features prominent in the context. The first is that the disciples are to witness in the world (15:26–27 and much of chapter 17). The Holy Spirit bears witness; *but the disciples must also witness.* In this sense, they join the Holy Spirit in preserving the presence of Christ in a Christ-rejecting world. The Spirit in part discharges his witnessing responsibility by transforming the believers. The second thing to observe is that although the passage is *about* the Spirit's ministry in the world, it is addressed *to* the disciples. The passage therefore simultaneously informs the believers what the Counsellor will do and assures them that they are not abandoned in their witness.

Putting these two together, it appears that Jesus is telling the disciples that although they are losing their opportunity to learn how to confront the world from the Master and his convicting ministry (for they see him no longer), nevertheless they are not being abandoned – because the Counsellor is coming and he will convict the world *by working in part through the believers.* The Holy Spirit convicts the world of its false righteousness because Jesus is returning to his Father and can no longer exercise this ministry; moreover, even though, with Jesus gone, the disciples can no longer observe him and thereby learn to duplicate this ministry, yet the Counsellor by his operation enables the disciples to bear witness with convicting force. Jesus' teaching on this subject should therefore greatly encourage his followers.

This interpretation is in conformity with the remarkable change in impact the disciples have after Pentecost. They do not particularly commend themselves during the earlier period; and their lives, ministry and conduct do not greatly serve to call the world to account. It is Jesus who at that time convicts the world of its righteousness; and it costs him his life. During the early years of the church's life, however, Jesus is no longer physically present; but his disciples, empowered by the Holy Spirit, take on the role of convicting the world of its righteousness. Now Peter stands up and with holy boldness declares, 'This man [Jesus] was handed over to you by God's set purpose and foreknowledge; and you, with the help of wicked men, put him to death by nailing him to the cross' (Acts 2:23). Or again: 'You handed him over to be killed, and you disowned him before Pilate, though he had decided to let him go. You disowned the Holy and Righteous One and asked that a murderer be released to you. You killed the author of life, but God raised him from the dead. We are witnesses of this' (Acts 3:13–15). When questioned, Peter, *filled with the Holy Spirit* (Acts 4:8), answers in much the same vein, convicting the rulers and elders of their false righteousness as evidenced by their treatment of Jesus. The disciples themselves pray for great boldness (Acts 4:29). Nor should it be thought that those first Christians convict the world by their words only. On the contrary: filled with the Spirit who wars against the flesh, they begin to produce the rich fruit of the Spirit in their lives (Gal. 5:22–25). Even slaves are instructed how to behave, how to conduct themselves as Christians. Inevitably, the conduct of believers begins to stand out against the backdrop of contemporary paganism. Men become divided not only by the Christians' prepositional witness but equally by their lives. In these ways the Holy Spirit, operating through the believers to produce deep, biblical righteousness, convicts the world of righteousness.

The Holy Spirit continues this ministry today. Whether in his own secret operation or through the believers he is actively transforming, he confronts the world with the inadequacy and even the corruption of its vaunted righteousness.

How tawdry is the world's righteousness when compared with that of Jesus! People hide so much. At every level of society there is so much veneer that the vileness of the corruption is hidden from open view. Not many human beings would want to expose their darkest thoughts to the gaze of their peers. The deep hatreds, silent blasphemies, recurrent doubts, pathetic lusts, cherished enmities and vain ambitions which crowd our minds are carefully screened off from the eye of contemporaries by rigorous adherence to acceptable conduct and cliché. The open journals of certain medieval mystics and Puritan pastors, men who often exposed their own dirty linen and struggled to be clean, are so perceptive and intense that they embarrass the modern generation (which, if it pursues religion at all, prefers the veneer of religious respectability). Sad to tell, this modern tendency can even be fostered by the stories of spectacular conversion to which we have become accustomed. By stressing the change effected at conversion, we sometimes imply, wittingly or unwittingly, that there is no remaining false righteousness to overcome.

As groups, societies, organizations, races and nations, we seem pledged to announce and defend our own righteousness. We trumpet aspects of our past which are truly commendable; but we hush up and cover the slovenly and dirty things we have done. Then we either writhe in self-doubt and secret guilt, or manufacture artificial rationales – structures of shoddy self-righteousness – instead of dragging into the open our false righteousness and asking for forgiveness. Into this accumulated self-justification, the Holy Spirit speaks his convicting word. In society, the Christian who is filled by the Spirit is to stand out as a person of integrity, humility and transparent righteousness, a person whose conduct points to a better standard and a more genuine righteousness than the world apart from Christ can ever attain.

The Counsellor, the Holy Spirit, also convicts the world of its judgment (16:8,11). This statement does not castigate only that judgment of the world which rejected Jesus, but all false judgment, of which the condemnation of Jesus is the supreme example. The world is wrong in its fundamental assessment of all things spiritual, and therefore primarily in its assessment of Jesus and his teaching and work. That is why Jesus at one point exhorts, 'Stop judging by mere appearances, and make a right judgment' (7:24). By contrast with the world's false judgment, Jesus' judgment is always just and right (5:30; 8:16).

Where the world's judgment is false, the error springs not from mere cognitive ignorance, but from moral perversity; not from an innocent confusion, but from a culpable willingness not to know. The Counsellor convicts the people of the world in this area of their thought; for unless they come to grips with their false judgments of spiritual reality, how shall they ever come to know him who is the truth? He is dismissed in advance by a culpable false judgment.

The Holy Spirit convicts the world of its judgment 'because the prince of this world now stands condemned' (16:11). Speaking proleptically of the cross, Jesus had earlier said, 'Now is the time for judgment on this world; now the prince of this world will be driven out' (12:31). The world thinks of the cross as the place where Jesus is condemned, but Jesus insists that in reality it is the place where the world is condemned and the prince of this world is decisively defeated. That victory heralds the inauguration of the eschatological age of blessing: believers enjoy eternal life right now, in the present, even if the consummation of that life awaits Christ's return. But by the same token, that victory on the cross also heralds the inauguration of the eschatological judgment: unbelievers already stand under the wrath and curse of God, even if the culmination of that curse awaits the last judgment. 'Whoever does not believe stands condemned already' (3:18); indeed, 'Whoever rejects the Son will not see life, for God's wrath remains on him' (3:36).

The cross-work of Jesus Christ is the crucial turning-point in the history of redemption. As it is the basis of the believer's salvation, so also is it the pivotal defeat of the prince of this world. As a result, the eschatological age is upon us: everything is immensely urgent. In the light of this eschatological urgency – that is, in the light of the fact that the devil already stands judged – the Counsellor convicts the world of its judgment. Here the world is in utter error in its fundamental assessment, while the most important judgment in the universe takes place under its very eyes, unobserved, in the cross and resurrection of Jesus. The 'today' of God's salvation has dawned (cf. Heb. 3:12–15); and therefore it is imperative that the world become aware of its false judgment. To this end the Holy Spirit is busy convicting the world.

There is a divine irony in this convicting work of the Holy Spirit. He convicts the world of its sin, when, because the world does not believe Jesus, it judges Jesus to be a sinner; 'We know this man [Jesus] is a sinner'

(9:24), the Jews affirm, and conspire to see him die the death of a common criminal. In fact, the world is so depraved it fails to discern what sin, righteousness and judgment really are; and only by the Spirit's deep, convicting work can the world hope to recognize the magnitude of its misconceptions and gross unbelief.

But this passage does more than explain something of the Counsellor's operation in the world. It serves also to foster quiet confidence in the heart of the believer as he faces his responsibility to witness. We look around at the world, and wonder how we can ever persuade men to believe the gospel of Jesus Christ. We do not want to stoop to gimmicks; and we perceive that intellectual argument alone guarantees nothing. We meet men and women who believe certain facts about Christianity, but who refuse to trust Christ; and we wonder how to penetrate the barrier of unbelief.

This uncertainty must have been especially acute among those first believers in the days immediately following the resurrection. To bear the responsibility for discharging the Great Commission must have seemed in some respects ridiculous to that little band. Certainly they forged no long-range policies, established no priority list of target countries and peoples, founded no training schools. Rather, they did what Jesus told them to do: they waited for the Spirit. When he came, he transformed the believers; and the believers then multiplied and spread, less out of dogged commitment than triumphant and holy enthusiasm.

I would quit all forms of Christian ministry immediately if I were not convinced that the Lord Jesus is building his church; that the Father has given over a people to his Son; and that the blessed Holy Spirit is working in the world to convict it of its sin, its righteousness and its judgment. I have no confidence that on my own I could

successfully persuade anyone of his deepest need and of
the truth of the gospel. And so the passage reassures
believers today that, far from being abandoned to their
task of witness, in fact they are privileged to be the chosen instruments by which the Spirit customarily performs his ministry. Such a perspective invests our labour
with a transcendent significance and obliterates the fear
of failure.

There is a second ministry of the Holy Spirit which
Jesus now further elucidates.

The Holy Spirit, the Paraclete, comes to the disciples in the absence of Jesus, to complete the revelation of the triune God in Jesus Christ (16:12–25)

'I have much more to say to you,' Jesus tells his disciples,
'more than you can now bear' (16:12). They cannot bear
more because of two factors: first, the crucial events, the
cross and the resurrection, had not yet taken place, and
they could scarcely envisage them – let alone assess their
profound significance; and second, the disciples were,
spiritually, still far too immature.

The latter is a more common barrier to the verbal
communication of biblical truth than is often recognized.
A brand new believer with no heritage of Christian
teaching may ask, 'Just what do we mean when we say,
"Jesus is God"?' But he expects a far briefer and less
sophisticated response than the believer taking an
advanced Christology course in his fourth year at a
graduate seminary. There might be many more things
that could be said to the former brother; but he would
not be able to bear them. In the training of new believers, this principle needs always to be borne in mind.

In the Farewell Discourse Jesus prepares his men as much as possible for what lies ahead. Even if they cannot grasp everything he says, he knows that it will bear fruit in their lives when, after the events to which he points, they recall his teaching and recognize that not for a moment were circumstances utterly removed from divine control and purpose. Even so, he recognizes that there is only so much he can give them at the moment: they are simply unable to bear more. Therefore Jesus returns again to the ministry the Counsellor will have towards the disciples in the future, a theme introduced earlier (14:25–26). Three truths are set forth.

1. The Counsellor comes to complete the revelation of God in Jesus Christ. 'But when he, the Spirit of truth, comes, he will guide you into all truth. He will not speak on his own; he will speak only what he hears, and he will tell you what is yet to come' (16:13).

Jesus has already promised that the Spirit of truth will remind the disciples of everything Jesus taught them (14:26). Now, he promises more: the Spirit will guide men into all truth, and tell them what is yet to come. That the Spirit will guide those first Christians into all truth does not mean, as we have already seen (chapter 4 of this book), that there is no need for teachers in the church, nor that finite human beings may enjoy omniscience. Rather, it is assurance that the disciples will be led into true understanding of the saving events taking place. Moreover, they will be afforded glimpses into the future. The final apocalyptic climax of world history will be partially unveiled before their eyes to enable them to perceive the sweep of the divine plan of redemption and the crucial place of Jesus within it. That will bring glory to Jesus (16:14, on which see below).

There is promise here of further revelation – indeed, of *propositional* revelation, revelation that is not merely a naked and unexplained event, but content that can be expressed in propositions. The Spirit will 'speak' and 'tell' the disciples what is coming. This should not be thought surprising, unless we think God is inarticulate. The Scriptures insist both that he is capable of speech, and that he speaks: is it any wonder he chooses to reveal himself propositionally to the one species he created on earth with full powers of speech and with the image and likeness of Deity stamped on its nature? As God *spoke* in times past through the prophets, and *spoke* through the Son, designated the *Word*, who *said* only what the Father gave him *to say*, so too he *spoke* by his Spirit, who completes the revelation of God in the Son by *speaking* and *telling* the disciples divine truth.

Implicitly, here is an anticipation of what we now call the New Testament canon. The time would come when a converted Jew by the name of Paul would set pen to paper, and many of his letters would be recognized as Scripture (2 Pet. 3:15–16). A physician named Luke would write one quarter of the New Testament. Others would contribute, including a half-brother of Jesus called James, who was at this time still an unbeliever. More revelation was necessary to unpack the glorious significance of the things taking place; and this ministry was to be discharged by the Holy Spirit.

2. *The Counsellor in his revelatory mission, Jesus says, will be as dependent on Jesus' as Jesus in the days of his flesh was dependent on his Father*. 'He will not speak on his own,' Jesus insists; 'he will speak only what he hears . . . He will bring glory to me by taking from what is mine and making it known to you. All that belongs to the Father is mine. That is why I said the Spirit will

take from what is mine and make it known to you' (16:13–15).

All along, Jesus has insisted that he has not spoken on his own, but has said only what the Father wanted him to say (cf. 7:17; 12:49; 14:10; chapter 2 of this book). This stance not only reflects Jesus' dependence upon and obedience to the Father, but, equally important, it guarantees that what he says is divine and in perfect harmony with the Father's will. Now the Spirit will guide the disciples; and Jesus says the Spirit, too, will not speak on his own. Rather, the Spirit will depend on what he hears for what he has to say. The teaching of the Spirit is, like the teaching of Jesus, nothing less than the teaching of God.

Moreover, the Spirit's general subject-matter is somewhat restricted; but it is a glorious restriction. The Spirit will take from what is Christ's and make it known to Christ's disciples. This curious phrasing succeeds in getting across three ideas:

First, the focus is entirely on Christ. The Spirit does not ramble on about any old subject, nor does he compete with the Son. The Spirit's role is to complete the revelation of God in Jesus Christ.

Second, the preposition *from* in the expression '*from* what is mine' (16:14–15) shows that the revelation the Spirit provides to Christians is not the entire sum of truth surrounding Christ. Finite human beings could not apprehend it even if it were given. Rather, the Spirit takes from this infinite sum and gives that truth to the disciples.

Third, if the Spirit does not speak on his own, but does speak the things that pertain to Christ – his person, his mission, his teaching – and if this be reflected in the New Testament, then the fundamental unity of the New Testament turns on Christ. Christ is the centre which gives these books their unity. 'In the past God spoke to our forefathers through the prophets at many times and in various ways,' writes the author of the Epistle to the Hebrews, 'but in these last days *he has spoken to us by his Son*' (Heb. 1:1–2*a*). The Son-revelation is the burden of the New Testament writers, who, inspired by the Holy Spirit, do not see themselves as *adding* to the revelation of Jesus himself, or *succeeding* it with new material, but merely *explaining* and spelling out propositionally the implications of that personal revelation.

3. The Holy Spirit's role is to bring glory to Jesus. This is explicitly affirmed: 'He will bring glory to me by taking from what is mine and making it known to you' (16:14). It was necessary for Jesus to be glorified – that is, to return to his Father's glorious presence by way of the cross, resurrection and exaltation – before the Spirit could be given (7:39); but once he is thus glorified, he receives yet more glory by the Spirit's ministry among the believers.

Nothing brings more glory to our exalted Lord Jesus than for his followers to become steeped in all truth concerning him. The acquisition of this knowledge, though intellectual, is not merely intellectual: as God's truth is truly absorbed by believers it transforms them, enabling them to reflect the Lord's glory and thereby bring praise to his name. As Paul puts it, 'And we, who with unveiled faces all reflect the Lord's glory, are being transformed into his likeness with ever-increasing glory, which comes from the Lord, who is the Spirit' (2 Cor. 3:18). Glory comes to Jesus as the truths of the gospel are established in the lives of men.

Christians today ought therefore to avoid two sad extremes. One extreme depreciates any sturdy study of biblical truth, dismissing it as unspiritual, and preferring to shout loud praises with worked-up responses and clichés – as if the magnitude of the glory we offer Jesus turns on decibel levels (or the depth of ignorance masked by self-professed faith). The other extreme depreciates spontaneous joy in worship and all corporate enthusiasm, dismissing such things as mere emotion, and preferring solemn and distinctively intellectual contemplation of propositions about Jesus – as if the magnitude of the glory we offer Jesus turns exclusively on how many truths the mind can formulate. In the context of John 16:12–15, it is the former error which receives shorter shrift; but in the context of the Bible as a whole, we who are believers must learn to glorify Jesus by increasingly apprehending as much graciously revealed truth as we can, forging it into our lives until it both transforms us and prompts spontaneous and enthusiastic praise. Away with wilfully ignorant clamour; away with arid truth intellectually appropriated but never absorbed or implemented.

In one sense, the Holy Spirit occupies a secondary place in the New Testament. The centre stage is enjoyed by Jesus Christ. But the Holy Spirit is not an optional extra. He is presented to us as an integral part of the divine plan of redemption, as essential to our salvation as the Father, as essential as Jesus. How could it be otherwise? There is but one God. If the Persons of the Godhead decreed in the harmony of their eternal counsel that the Son should become a man, that he alone should be the sacrificial Lamb to expiate our sins, they did not by this decision abandon him to his work. There is but one God; and this triune God effects all the counsels of his undivided will. It is impossible to imagine how the New Testament presentation of salvation could remain intact if prominent place were not reserved for the ministries of *each* of the Persons of the Godhead.

In John 16:5–15, attention is directed primarily to two specific ministries of the Holy Spirit. For these clarifications, we are profoundly grateful. They fit into the broader picture of the Spirit's person and ministry scattered throughout the pages of the New Testament books, a picture which prompts believers to sing and pray:

> Our blessed Redeemer, ere He breathed
>   His tender, last farewell,
> A Guide, a Comforter bequeathed
>   With us to dwell.
>
> He came in semblance of a dove,
>   With sheltering wings outspread,
> The holy balm of peace and love
>   On earth to shed.
>
> He came in tongues of living flame
>   To teach, convince, subdue;
> All-powerful as the wind He came,
>   As viewless too.
>
> And His that gentle voice we hear,
>   Soft as the breath of even,
> That checks each fault, that calms each fear,
>   And speaks of heaven.
>
> And every virtue we possess,
>   And every victory won.
> And every thought of holiness
>   Are His alone.
>
> Spirit of purity and grace,
>   Our weakness, pitying, see;
> O make our hearts Thy dwelling-place,
>   And worthier Thee.
>
> *Harriet Auber (1773–1862)*

8 (John 16:16–33)

But First, the Cross

'In a little while you will see me no more, and then after
a little while you will see me.'

Some of his disciples said to one another, 'What does
he mean by saying, "In a little while you will see me no
more, and then after a little while you will see me," and
"Because I am going to the Father"?' They kept asking,
'What does he mean by "a little while"? We don't understand what he is saying.'

Jesus saw that they wanted to ask him about this, so
he said to them, 'Are you asking one another what I
meant when I said, "In a little white you will see me no
more, and then after a little while you will see me"? I
tell you the truth, you will weep and mourn while the
world rejoices. You will grieve, but your grief will turn
to joy. A woman giving birth to a child has pain
because her time has come; but when her baby is born
she forgets the anguish because of her joy that a child
is born into the world, So with you: Now is your time
of grief, but I will see you again and you will rejoice,
and no-one will take away your joy. In that day you
will no longer ask me anything. I tell you the truth, my
Father will give you whatever you ask in my name.

Until now you have not asked for anything in my name. Ask and you will receive, and your joy will be complete.

'Though I have been speaking figuratively, a time is coming when I will no longer use this kind of language but will tell you plainly about my Father. In that day you will ask in my name. I am not saying that I will ask the Father on your behalf. No, the Father himself loves you because you have loved me and have believed that I came from God. I came from the Father and entered the world; now I am leaving the world and going back to the Father.'

Then Jesus' disciples said, 'Now you are speaking clearly and without figures of speech. Now we can see that you know all things and that you do not even need to have anyone ask you questions. This makes us believe that you came from God.'

'You believe at last!' Jesus answered. 'But a time is coming, and has come, when you will be scattered, each to his own home. You will leave me all alone. Yet I am not alone, for my Father is with me.

'I have told you these things, so that in me you may have peace. In this world you will have trouble. But take heart! I have overcome the world.'

Picturing the scene is not easy. Are Jesus and his eleven disciples still making their way along narrow streets and paths towards the Kidron Valley? Are the men clumping together in little groups of various combinations as the confines of the way rearrange them again and again? Is this what prompts the questions to flit around the group? Perhaps so; it is difficult to be certain of the physical setting at this point.

Nevertheless, the conceptual setting is not so ambiguous. Jesus has been allaying the fears of his followers.

These men recognize that Jesus is about to leave, and that he has been speaking about betrayal and death, yet also about returning to his Father. Jesus has been using this opportunity to instruct his men on some of the long-range implications of his imminent departure. He has told them about his provision of another Counsellor, the Holy Spirit. Some of the Spirit's special ministries Jesus has outlined in some detail; and repeatedly he has tied together the Father, the Spirit and himself in a relationship which allows distinctions yet which demands unity.

Clearly, Jesus wants to assure his men that, despite his departure, every contingency has been recognized and plans for their well-being have been established. His departure itself effects a new relationship with God for these believers; and they will enjoy a spiritual intimacy with the exalted Christ that issues in fruitfulness, triumphant prayer, and joyful, loving obedience. It is true, of course, that they will face opposition, persecution, and even torture and death; but this is part of following Jesus, and in any case it is the path taken by Jesus himself. The disciples, Jesus makes clear, are to stay behind after Jesus' departure to bear witness to the world; but even so, they will be joined by the Holy Spirit who himself will be working to bear witness and convict the world.

Even if the disciples find themselves unable to grasp all that Jesus is telling them, they perceive that he is promising further explanation once the Counsellor comes. One of the Counsellor's prime responsibilities will be to unravel a little further for the disciples the full significance of Jesus Christ. To be exposed to this fullness of revelation is to receive instruction of unimaginable worth and unprecedented privilege; it stamps believers as the friends of Jesus Christ.

These, in brief, are some of the major themes with which Jesus has been dealing in this Farewell Discourse. The scale of the discussion is epic. Much of what he has said Jesus has related directly or indirectly to the cross, now looming close: for instance, the Holy Spirit cannot come until Jesus 'goes' (to the Father via the cross), and his 'going' is for the disciples' good. Throughout, Jesus has provided something of a panoramic perspective that looks into the future and glimpses the sweep of the divine plan of redemption. But the one thing with which Jesus has not yet dealt is the immediate crisis of the cross – the crisis, that is to say, that the disciples will face when for three days Jesus will be dead, the resurrection still unknown, the Holy Spirit still not sent.

It is true that the Counsellor, the blessed Spirit of truth, will be sent to the disciples; but first, the cross. It is true that the disciples will learn to serve as witnesses in a hostile world; but first, the cross. They will, of course, enter into deep, spiritual intimacy with the exalted Lord; but first, the cross. More revelation will be given by the coming Holy Spirit; but first, the cross. And so it is to the cross, this crucial saving appointment, that Jesus now turns his attention. Even so, he deals with it less from the perspective of salvation history, or from his own vantage-point of suffering, torment and rejection, than from the point of view of his disciples who will face profound grief and confusion during the next three days. Therefore he says, 'In a little while you will see me no more, and then after a little while you will see me' (16:16).

It must be admitted that many commentators think that this verse (16:16) refers to Jesus' absence during the period from the ascension to the parousia (compare the language in 14:19,28). Others hold that it refers to Jesus' personal 'going away' bodily and his return by means of the promised Counsellor (compare 14:23). Still others hold that the language is purposely ambiguous, and that Jesus' departure is phrased in this unclear fashion in order to suggest that the one departure/return is a type of all of them.

There are, however, several indications which argue strongly that the passage is not so complex: it refers simply to Jesus' departure by the death of the cross and his return by resurrection. The following points should be noted: (1) Only John 16:16 adds the phrase 'after a little while' to the promise 'you will see me'. This is not accidental. (2) The picture of the disciples weeping and mourning while the world rejoices (16:20) fits *only* the period during which Jesus is in the grave. After the resurrection, John is careful to point out, the 'disciples were overjoyed when they saw the Lord' (20:20). Acts attests that the early Christians after Pentecost experienced great joy (Acts 13:52; cf. 5:41; 16:25). Only while Jesus' body lay in the tomb were the disciples overwhelmed with grief. (3) The analogy of the woman giving birth likewise fits best into the sharp, short agony of the three-day period immediately ahead. (4) This interpretation fits best into the Farewell Discourse. Jesus' departure and subsequent return at the parousia have already been treated, as also has his return by the Spirit; but so far Jesus has said nothing unambiguous about the three-day departure into death. It is fitting to bring the Farewell Discourse to a close by focusing on Christ's passion and death: apart from the prayer of John 17, the passion and death are the next events to ensue.

This one verse, John 16:16, leads to an extended discussion with five main interlocking but developing themes; and over all of them hangs the shadow of the cross.

The threatened departure of Jesus prompts confusion among Jesus' disciples (16:17–18)

'Some of his disciples said to one another, "What does he mean by saying, 'In a little while you will see me no more, and then after a little while you will see me,' and 'Because I am going to the Father'?" They kept asking, "What does he mean by 'a little while'? We don't understand what he is saying"' (16:17–18).

The disciples focus their attention on the phrase 'in a little while'. By this time they know Jesus is leaving; but they still have not sorted out the various returns he would make – the return at the resurrection, the return by the Holy Spirit, the return at the parousia. Therefore they make the natural mistake: they not only confuse these various stages of Jesus' return, but in focusing on the new phrase, 'in a little while', they read this phrase into the complexities surrounding Christ's return and thereby fail entirely to restrict the phrase to the resurrection return. They understand this statement in the light of his earlier clause, 'Because I am going to the Father' (16:10).

Of course, we should not be surprised by their misunderstanding. The reason Jesus was giving all this material was not to lay out a detailed blueprint for the future, but to give them enough of an outline that after the events they would come to recognize that Jesus himself knew what was going to transpire. Indeed, one of the strongest arguments for the authenticity of the contents of these three chapters (John 14 to 16) is their ambiguity. Theologically they are direct and clear; but in referring to historical events placed *ahead* of the Discourse, they are amazingly sketchy. Someone who was out to manufacture a Farewell Discourse after the events would in all likelihood have succumbed to the

temptation to be far more precise than Jesus in the days
of his flesh often chose to be.

The picture one forms of 16:17–18 is of small groups
of disciples passing their questions among themselves
as the entire body winds its way down the lanes.
Whispering, gesticulating, wondering, they cannot
understand what Jesus means by 'a little while' and
how the phrase fits into the rest of what he has said.
Why they do not ask Jesus is unclear. Perhaps they feel
their questions have revealed enough ignorance for one
night, and this one they will try to sort out on their own.
John does not record any reason. All he makes clear is
that the minds of the disciples are full of confusion at
this point.

In one sense, that is comforting. As believers grow,
they sometimes come across difficult truths or painful
experiences which for a sustained period they cannot
understand. Even mature and well-trained believers
sometimes find themselves in water over their heads.
God is not finished with us after we have been
Christians six months, or three years, or fifty years.
There is still so much to learn; so much to understand.
We may not face Jesus' physical departure as did those
first disciples; but many a senior saint can testify to
experiences in which he has felt utterly abandoned. We
may then be tempted to read the Word of God and
protest, 'We don't understand what he is saying.' It is
this sense of personal loss and abandonment which
breeds confusion.

Yet we must be careful to preserve the historical
uniqueness of the confusion of the disciples at this point.
They do not yet grieve very much: they are confused
and uncertain, but not yet in tears. The threatened
departure of Jesus is still only threat: it generates confusion.

The confusion thus prompted will turn to grief, and the grief will turn to joy (16:19–24)

There are three important points to note in this paragraph:

The first is that Jesus replies to their need, rather than to their question. Their question is phrased in terms of understanding what Jesus has said; but Jesus discerns that their deepest concern is his departure, not the meaning of a phrase. They are upset, confused; but above all they are still ill-prepared for the acute grief that will be theirs.

Jesus forces them to face this impending grief squarely; but he goes on to assure them that they will pass through sorrow to joy. 'I tell you the truth,' he says, 'you will weep and mourn while the world rejoices. You will grieve, but your grief will turn to joy' (16:20). With this promise in their hearts, the deep sorrow that will pummel them in a few short hours will not be of the sort that generates panic. The promise will not eliminate their grief, and perhaps scarcely alleviate it; but it will stabilize the believers by providing a larger perspective.

Sometimes today the Lord Christ chooses to answer not our questions but our needs; and sometimes such an answer comes by the provision of a larger perspective. Like the heroes of faith in Hebrews 11, we are then able to endure as though seeing him who is invisible. We learn that temporary alienation will ultimately give way to the city with foundations whose architect and builder is God. Though we are foreigners and strangers on earth, we look for a better country – a heavenly one. We discover that tears endure for the night, but joy comes in the morning.

The second point to observe is that the disciples' sorrow is not simply *displaced* by joy, but rather their sorrow *turns into* joy. 'You will grieve,' Jesus says, 'but your grief *will turn to joy*' (16:20). The analogy Jesus selects makes the same point: 'A woman giving birth to a child has pain because her time has come; but when her baby is born she forgets the anguish because of her joy that a child is born into the world. So with you: Now is your time of grief, but I will see you again and you will rejoice, and no-one will take away your joy' (16:21–22). The very thing that generates the woman's grief, child-bearing, also generates her joy. So with the disciples: the thing that generates their grief, namely the cross, will ultimately prompt their joy. And their joy cannot be taken away.

We need this perspective in a vast array of circum-stances. At the most pedestrian level, we recognize both from Scripture and from experience that discipline imposed by a parent on a child is not usually appreciated by the child at the time (cf. Heb. 12:4ff.). Nevertheless that very chastening under which the child chafes he one day looks back upon with gratitude and appreciation. So also the discipline of the Lord. 'No discipline seems pleasant at the time, but painful. Later on, however, it produces a harvest of righteousness and peace for those who have been trained by it' (Heb. 12:11).

Many of our losses and griefs, though extraordinarily painful at the time, generate great spiritual growth and stable joy in our lives. So it was with the apostles.

Perhaps there is another implication bound up with the analogy of the woman giving birth to a child. This picture is used in Old Testament times to depict the woes which presage the Messianic salvation (e.g. Isa. 26:16–19; 66:7–14; Mic. 4:9–10). In the intertestamental period, this figure becomes very common, and rabbis spoke of 'the travail pains of the Messiah' (by which they referred to a period of trouble before the Messianic

age). Jesus' death/resurrection/exaltation is an eschatological event, in that it pronounces both ultimate judgment and ultimate justification; and so it is appropriate
that the Messianic age inaugurated by this eschatological event likewise be prefaced by a period of sharp
anguish. In one sense, of course, these things prefigure
the trouble which immediately precedes the *consummation* of the Messiah's salvation; but it is not inappropri-
ate to detect anguish before the *inauguration* of that
salvation. In any case, the anguish of the apostles is to be
turned into steadfast joy.

The third point to note is that two important blessings
are bound up with this joy. The first is fullness of understanding that will obviate the need to ask questions of
the sort they have been throwing at Jesus (13:24–25,37;
14:5,8,22; 16:17–18): 'In that day you will no longer ask
me anything' (16:23*a*). The verb here means 'ask a question' rather than 'ask for something'. In 'that day', once
Jesus has risen from the dead and the Holy Spirit has
been bequeathed, they will no longer need to ask the
questions with which they ply Jesus and demonstrate
their profound confusion. They will enjoy a fullness of
understanding which will swallow up their present confusion in joyful comprehension.

The second blessing, introduced as a new thought by
the words 'I tell you the truth', is ready access in Jesus'
name to the Father's prayer-answering power: 'I tell you
the truth, my Father will give you whatever you ask in
my name. Until now you have not asked for anything in
my name. Ask and you will receive, and your joy will be
complete' (16:23*b*–24). The disciples, Jesus says, have not
yet asked (God) for anything in Jesus' name. The verb
for 'ask' in this text means 'ask for something' rather
than 'ask a question': the thought has moved on from
16:23*a*. But the real stress lies on the phrase 'in my

name'. Of course, the disciples could not yet have asked for things in Jesus' name: the mediatorial role of Christ in this regard turns on his cross-work. Now, however, in anticipation of that completed work, they are invited to ask the Father for things – to ask in Jesus' name. The passage is reminiscent of 14:14 and 15:7–8,16 (on which see chapter 5 of this book); but in this context there is more stress on Jesus' mediatorial role and on the joy that is related to this fruitful prayer. By this means Jesus again promises his apostles that their impending grief will turn to joy.

The joy thus gained is bound up with the sheer delight of a personal knowledge of the Father's love (16:25–28)

At this point Jesus acknowledges that he has been speaking in a veiled way. He comments, 'Though I have been speaking figuratively [in context, "figuratively" does not mean "with figures of speech" but "with veiled speech", in contrast to the "plainly" at the end of the verse], a time is coming when I will no longer use this kind of language but will tell you plainly about my Father' (16:25).

According to Luke, that time of plain speech began with Jesus' post-resurrection appearances. Jesus began to explain to his followers 'what was said in all the Scriptures concerning himself' (Luke 24:27); and 'he opened their minds so they could understand the Scriptures' (Luke 24:45).

It is not as if in the post-resurrection period Jesus will introduce a new teaching or redefine his mission. Rather, he will explain more clearly what he has already explained. All along Jesus has been revealing the Father

(14:9; cf. 1:18); but the nature of his mission has precluded a more explicit detailing of the cross/resurrection/exaltation until that climactic event has taken place. At this point, his revelation of the Father would be more comprehensible to his followers.

Once that day has arrived, the believers will understand clearly what it means to ask the Father for things in Jesus' name. *'In that day'* Jesus says, 'you will ask in my name' (16:26*a*). As we have already seen, such privileged intercession is bound up with the joy the disciples will experience after Christ's resurrection (16:24, and comments, above). But there is a danger in stressing the use of Jesus' name in this new prayer-relationship with the Father: it might lead some to think, incorrectly, that the Father is standoffish and essentially alien to the followers of Jesus. This potential misconception Jesus therefore hastens to clear up: 'I am not saying that I will ask the Father on your behalf. No, the Father himself loves you because you have loved me and have believed that I came from God' (16:26*b*–27).

What the disciples must recognize is that their forthcoming privileges of intercession are not wheedled out of the Father by the intercession of the Son; rather, they are based on a loving relationship with the Father himself. Father and Son are at one in the plan of redemption. The Son's death/resurrection/exaltation, it is true, puts the divine plan into effect and establishes the ground – forgiveness of sin and removal of guilt – upon which this relationship with God is established. But we have already seen (14:23) that the Christian enjoys an intimate spiritual relationship with the triune God, not with the Spirit only or with the Son only.

This passage (16:26*b*–27) does not contradict other New Testament texts which picture the exalted Jesus interceding for his people (Rom. 8:34; Heb. 7:25; 1 John

2:1), since these passages have little to do with believers' prayerful petitions but rather are concerned with their status before God. That status rests exclusively upon the cross-work of Christ: as Priest and sacrifice, he offered himself as an offering to God for his people. Because of that work, we have free access to God; and therefore we pray 'in Jesus' name'. But that is something rather different from supposing that we pray to Jesus and then Jesus offers our petitions to his Father on our behalf. The truth of the matter is that Jesus' priestly ministry establishes our acceptance before God; and, once accepted, we enjoy ready privileges of direct petition 'in Jesus' name'.

The Father loves us (16:27): that is the wonderful truth we must learn. He loved us enough to send his Son; and now with the Son's cross-work a fact of history, and our offence to Deity's holiness removed by the Lamb of God, the Father loves us because we have loved Jesus. Therefore the joy gained by living this side of Calvary is unmistakably bound up with the sheer delight of a personal knowledge of the Father's love.

It is worth pausing to reflect a little further on this theme of joy in the Farewell Discourse. In 15:9–11, Jesus links the believer's joy to a personal relationship of obedience to Christ. The joy cannot be experienced without obedient commitment. Now, in 16:24ff., we discover further that the believer's joy turns in part on fruitful prayer uttered in Jesus' name, prayer which enjoys open access to the Father and is but a privileged response to the Father's love. It is essential to recognize that in both instances joy is linked with something else. Joy is not an independent gift, unrelated to other aspects of a believer's life.

What this means in practical terms is that the believer who expects bundles of joy to be showered upon him, regardless of the consistency of his relationship with Jesus and irrespective of his prayer life, is deluded. We are to believe Jesus Christ not because of an unqualified desire for joy, but because Christianity, biblically defined, is true: Jesus is who he claims to be, and he alone is the means by which our guilt before God may be set aside. Only by faith in Jesus Christ is there eternal life, personal knowledge of the Father, and the gift of the Holy Spirit. Christian truth is to be pursued and believed primarily for one reason: it is *truth*. But once committed to the truth of Christ, there are rich spin-offs in the coinage of joy. If Christian claims were untrue, then it should not be believed, *regardless of how much joy belief in untrue teaching might generate.*

We may look at this another way, and ask what things tend to foster personal joy. Our spiritual health may be assessed by our answers. If obedience to Christ makes us warm with joy, and if fruitful petitionary prayer to our loving God and Father completes our joy, then we are approximating Jesus' expectation of what his followers should experience this side of the cross. If obedience is distasteful and, when grudgingly pursued, the source of more dissatisfaction than joy; or if prayer, however difficult, always fails to evoke joy in the heart of the believer who disciplines himself to pray, then the medical alarms connected with spiritual health are sounding loudly.

John learnt this lesson well. Towards the end of his life he could write a letter which says in part, 'It has given me great joy to find some of your children walking in the truth, just as the Father commanded us' (2 John 4). Here the aged apostle is concerned that the truth of God advance, and that professing believers adhere to it unreservedly. He labours and prays and devotes himself to these ends; and so he experiences joy when he perceives that the truth of the gospel is truly transforming lives. In a similar vein, he writes to his dear friend Gaius: 'It gave me great joy to have some brothers come and tell about your faithfulness to the truth and how you continue to walk in the truth. I have no greater joy than to hear that my children are walking in the truth' (3 John 3–4).

The Christian's joy in the Lord is bound up with the Lord. Nothing will nourish his joy as much as a growing desire to please Christ, a developing faithfulness in prayer, a deepening awareness of the Father's fathomless love.

Jesus' disciples can easily abuse these truths and falsely assess themselves in their light (16:29–32)

'Then Jesus' disciples said, "Now you are speaking clearly and without figures of speech [i.e., veiled speech]. Now we can see that you know all things and that you do not even need to have anyone ask you questions. This makes us believe that you came from God"' (16:29–30).

Some people bluff their way through life. Several years ago on Canadian television an interviewer asked several people on the streets of downtown Winnipeg what they thought of the political performance of D'Arcy McGee as a cabinet minister. The interviewer neglected to mention that McGee died in the last century (7 April 1868); so the passers-by not unnaturally thought they were being asked about the performance of a current political figure. But only a few admitted they did not have a clue who McGee was. Most replied with answers like these: 'Oh, he's all right, I guess – for a liberal'; or, 'Terrible, just terrible. But he's not as bad as —'; or, better yet, 'I saw him the other night on television; but I haven't really decided about him yet.'

In an age when knowledge is power, no-one wants to admit ignorance. Even home Bible studies produce their share of bluffers. Someone remarks that the propitiation Christ effected must surely turn on the unique, ontological Sonship of Christ – doesn't everyone agree? And immediately heads nod wisely, even those who have no idea what *propitiation* and *ontological* mean. Academics are not exempt from this sin: how many will admit, when they are asked whether they have read a certain new volume that lies within the realm of their specialist interest, that they have not even heard of the title?

In all fairness, Jesus' disciples are not as bad as that. They are certainly not out-and-out liars. However, they do claim to know more than they actually know. Jesus' statements in 16:27–28 they claim to believe and understand. How little they really understand Jesus quickly points out; but we may set aside his rebuke for a moment and try to understand just what the disciples claim they have grasped.

What makes the disciples believe that Jesus came from God is that he does not need to have anyone ask him questions (16:30). It appears that the disciples have been taken aback by Jesus' ability to discern their questions before they utter them (cf. 16:30). Earlier in this Gospel, Jesus exhibits his ability to know what is on the minds of certain people (1:47,50; 4:19,29); and among many Jews such ability was thought to signify something of the divine. The Jewish historian Josephus, for instance, ascribes to the lips of Jonathan the words: 'This God . . . who, before I have expressed my thought in words, already knows what it is' (*Antiquities* vi. 230). Did not Jesus himself teach, 'Your Father knows what you need before you ask him' (Matt. 6:8)? Therefore if Jesus demonstrates this ability, it is quite clear that he must have come from God: such, at least, is the reasoning of the disciples in 16:30.

In one sense, of course, the disciples are quite right. They here offer a true confession of faith. They utter nothing false, nothing heterodox; and they are slowly arriving at a more accurate understanding of who Jesus is.

Nevertheless, their confession must be faulted on two grounds. First of all, they have focused their attention on what is perhaps the least significant aspect of what Jesus has said. They seize upon his ability to anticipate their questions. They have not begun to grasp the essential content of what Jesus has been saying. Moreover, they exhibit an even more serious fault: they assess themselves highly on the basis of their one true insight. 'Now you are speaking clearly . . . Now we can see . . . ,' they claim, with a touch of self-satisfaction.

'You believe at last!' Jesus answers (16:31), with gentle irony; or perhaps the text should be read as a question, 'Do you now believe?' Either way, the inadequacy of their belief is revealed in Jesus' next words. As he looks to Gethsemane and the cross, now immediately ahead, Jesus says to them, 'But a time is coming, and has come, when you will be scattered, each to his own home. You will leave me all alone. Yet I am not alone, for my Father is with me' (16:32). The disciples do believe, after a fashion; but they have leapt to the illegitimate conclusion that they really understand Jesus' meaning, even before the death/resurrection/exaltation of Jesus and before the coming of the Spirit and the revelation he will bring. Jesus answers by predicting the shameful scattering which will prove conclusively how little they truly grasp – in short, how little they understand both of the truth and of themselves.

In one sense, of course, the problem the disciples face is unique. Their failure to grasp all that Jesus is saying depends in part on the fact that they are living at the

turn of the ages, during that amazing period when the
Mosaic covenant was becoming obsolete and giving
way to the new covenant, when the climactic event of
the cross/resurrection/exaltation had not yet taken
place and could scarcely be envisaged. 'But first, the
cross': in that sense, their failures at this point are unrepeatable. In another sense, however, we modern believers sometimes prove adept at duplicating the faults of
the first followers of Jesus – the faults in John 16 not
excluded.

For instance, we may focus our theological attention
on relatively minor points and miss the sweep and glory
of biblical truth. We may think our understanding is far
more mature and sophisticated than it really is. Even our
true confessions may be hopelessly compromised by
such spiritual immaturity that they cannot stand the
assault of severe disappointment, opposition, bereave-
ment, or pain.

At the same time, it is comforting to recognize that the
entire apostolic band was made up of believers of this
order; yet God in his mercy and gracious timing ultimately transformed them into men who turned their
world upside-down for Jesus Christ. This very poor
beginning serves to remind us that Christianity owes its
genesis not to the apostles but to Christ; and this lesson
must be learnt afresh in every generation. C.H. Dodd
comments insightfully: 'It is part of the character and
genius of the Church that its foundation members were
discredited men; it owed its existence not to their faith,
courage, or virtue, but to what Christ had done with
them; and this they could never forget.' Leon Morris
adds, 'The church depends ultimately on what God has
done in Christ, not on the courage and wit of its first
members.' What is essential for us today is to know
him and believe him increasingly, while avoiding any

suggestion that the little knowledge and faith we do possess make us spiritual stalwarts or supersaints.

Precisely because the cross/resurrection/exaltation depends on the divine plan, not on Christ's followers, Jesus is able to add, 'You will leave me all alone. Yet I am not alone, for my Father is with me' (16:32*b*). And so Jesus prepares to go to the cross – while his followers rate themselves highly on some spiritual scale, and continue in their failure to comprehend the greatest self-sacrifice conceivable.

Invitation to faith: outlook on the world from the perspective of Jesus' triumph (16:33)

Why has Jesus given all this material (John 14 to 16) to his disciples? 'I have told you these things,' he says, 'so that in me you may have peace' (16:33*a*).

This peace will come about in several different ways. First, because Jesus outlines what will take place in advance of the crucial saving events, therefore when those events occur the disciples will be forced to recognize that Jesus is in control. Once they come to that point, all of this instruction will confirm his truthfulness to them and thereby increase their faith. Moreover, after the resurrection they will be tormented by remorse and guilt. Here, too, Jesus has paved the way for their ultimate peace by forcing them to live in Jesus.

Again, Jesus has foretold of the persecutions they will endure, and he reminds them of these things again: 'In this world you will have trouble.' But by setting forth the true dimensions of such trouble (especially in 15:18 – 16:4), Jesus is ensuring their peace.

The Farewell Discourse has thus come full circle. At the beginning, Jesus' followers are told 'Do not let your hearts be troubled. Trust in God; trust also in me' (14:1). Now we read again: 'In this world you will have trouble. But take heart! I have overcome the world' (16:33). Both of these texts focus on Jesus Christ. Both of them promise peace to the believer who truly trusts Christ. In one sense, all of the Farewell Discourse has been about Christ. Therefore all that Jesus has been saying is to encourage his followers to look at the world from the perspective of Jesus and its triumph.

What does the world look like from the perspective of Jesus' triumphant death/resurrection/exaltation? On the one hand the world appears all the more evil and loathsome; yet, on the other hand, this is the world the Father loved enough to send his Son, the world for which the Lamb of God died. On the one hand, this is the world that rejected the Saviour and condemned him to death; yet, on the other hand, by that same death the Saviour defeated the prince of this world. On the one hand, this is the world which persecutes God's people and inflicts both petty irritants and massive scourges upon them; yet, on the other hand, that is the way the Master went, and therefore it is the way his disciples must be prepared to go. On the one hand, the world spells trouble; but on the other hand, living by faith in Jesus enables us to partake of the age to come and thereby serve and grow as members of eschatological community transported into time. The crucial victory has been fought; Jesus has overcome: 'Be of good cheer; I have overcome the world.' We live and love and serve while waiting for his triumphant return.

It is most important that believers develop the right perspectives. The world seen from the perspective of Jesus' cross/resurrection/exaltation appears to be a very different place from the one we picture without the advantage of this perspective.

Perspectives

The hurts of a grim weary world, the greeds of an all-
  selfish race,
The barbs fueled with malice and hurled by men void of
  vision and grace;
The children who die without food, still others ripped
  out from the womb,
Cheap culture defended as good near ghettoes of filth,
  rats and gloom;
Armed missiles with power to melt the shiny new toys
  that we buy,
The alien fear that is felt by people too guilty to die;
The endless, vain idols of men, the worship of fleeting
  applause,
The dollar, the Deutschemark, the yen as bases of
  wisdom and laws;
Religion that pampers to self, and cares not a whit for the
  damned,
The elderly put on the shelf, and truth manufactured
  and canned –
O Christ! These are ugly, deep stains and festering sores.
  This decay
Conspires to call forth refrains of defeat, gross self-pity,
  delay.
Responses by men seem so frail, and freighted with
  motives quite mixed.
Solutions of promise soon fail; the cries of Cassandra
  now fixed
In mem'ries that once thought she lied prompt fear and
  despair in the few;
But new generations, untried, can scoff at her warnings
  anew.
We'll build a new world, they proclaim: and new
  despots come to the throne.

The wearisome cycle again. The new god is yesterday's
     clone.

The vision we need to transcend this cyclical pattern of
     wrong
Looks back in the history of men, and forward to time's
     setting sun.
To gaze at Golgotha provides unshakable vantage of view:
Creator of time in its tides; the Judge standing under
     review;
The incarnate Lover, alone; bright Glory enshrouded in
     gray;
Perfection that wills to atone; and Grace by rejection
     repaid.

Yet forward our gaze is drawn, too. Spectacular vistas
     are spread;
The Living One whom we once slew now speaks, and
     his voice wakes the dead.
And him we scorned sits to receive the worship that is
     but his due;
And him we thought false, we perceive to be titled The
     Faithful and True.
The Crucified now stands as Judge; his justice no man
     can gainsay;
And only his death can expunge the multiplied sins of
     our way.
The earth and its heaven cannot stand before his pure
     unshaded light;
But these are remade by his hand, evoking unbounded
delight.
The dark shades are no longer seen, and untainted
     purity reigns;
And gracing the whole is a stream of unbroken,
     unrestrained praise.

Grant, gracious Savior, we pray, perspectives as seen
    from your throne:
Our world and our deep, wicked way, yet cherished and
    not left alone:
Between the glad grief of the Cross, and cosmic renewal
    to come
To serve you afresh at all cost, to sing now eternity's
    song.

'I have told you these things, so that in me you may have
peace. In this world you will have trouble. But take
heart! I have overcome the world' (16:33).

9 (John 17:1–19)

Jesus Prays for Himself and for His Followers

After Jesus said this, he looked towards heaven and prayed:

'Father, the time has come. Glorify your Son, that your Son may glorify you. For you granted him authority over all people that he might give eternal life to all those you have given him. Now this is eternal life: that they may know you, the only true God, and Jesus Christ, whom you have sent. I have brought you glory on earth by completing the work you gave me to do. And now, Father, glorify me in your presence with the glory I had with you before the world began.

'I have revealed you to those whom you gave me out of the world. They were yours; you gave them to me and they have obeyed your word. Now they know that everything you have given me comes from you. For I gave them the words you gave me and they accepted them. They knew with certainty that I came from you, and they believed that you sent me. I pray for them. I am not praying for the world, but for those you have given me, for they are yours. All I have is yours, and all you have is mine. And glory has come to me through them. I will remain in the world no longer, but they are still in the world, and I am coming to you. Holy Father, protect them by the power of your name – the name you gave me – so that they may be one as we are one. While I was with them, I protected them and kept them safe by that name you gave me. None has been lost except the one doomed to destruction so that Scripture would be fulfilled.

'I am coming to you now, but I say these things while I am still in the world, so that they may have the full measure of my joy within them. I have given them your word and the world has hated them, for they are not of the world any more than I am of the world. My prayer is not that you take them out of the world but that you protect them from the evil one. They are not of the world, even as I am not of it. Sanctify them by the truth; your word is truth. As you sent me into the world, I have sent them into the world. For them I sanctify myself, that they too may be truly sanctified.'

Traditionally, Christians have long referred to John 17 as the 'High Priestly Prayer' offered up by Jesus just before his passion. This is something of a misnomer, primarily because the themes in John 17 are too broad to be restricted to this priestly category. Ideally, we might refer to this prayer simply as 'the Lord's prayer', were it not for the fact that this rubric has traditionally been applied to what might better be called 'the Lord's model prayer' (Matt. 6:9–13; Luke 11:2–4).

At least a few parallels stand out between the prayer Jesus taught his disciples to pray and this prayer which Jesus himself prayed. The expression 'Our Father' is reflected here in the simple 'Father' (17:1). 'Hallowed be your *name*' may find some echo in the mention of God's *name* in 17:6,11–12,26 (only 17:11–12 in the NIV: see the exposition below). 'Your kingdom come' has certain thematic connections with 'glorify your Son' (17:1,5). We might also compare 'lead us not into temptation' with 'I protected them and kept them safe' (17:12), and 'deliver us from the evil one' with 'protect them from the evil one' (17:15).

Of course there are many differences; but the similarities suggest, at least, that the one who prays in John 17 has already become familiar to us by the model prayer he taught his disciples to pray.

Jesus' habit of praying is mentioned frequently by the Gospel writers, more so by Luke than by the others (cf. Matt. 11:25–26; Mark 1:35; 6:46; Luke 3:21; 5:16; 6:12; 9:18,28; 11:1; 22:42; 23:34,46; John 11:41; 12:27). Only rarely, how-ever, is the content of his prayer given; and when it is, it is usually short and pithy (e.g. Matt. 11:25–26; John 11:41). Occasions when Jesus prays at length are noted by the Evangelists; but ordinarily Jesus prayed alone when he prayed at length. Hence John 17 is a remarkable exception: Jesus here prays at some length, yet in the presence of witnesses. And Jesus is conscious that, although he is praying to the Father, he is praying so that his followers can hear what he is saying (see on 17:13, below).

The chapter opens with the introduction, 'After Jesus said this, he looked towards heaven and prayed.' The 'this' refers to the entire Farewell Discourse; and so we are to understand that this final prayer is the capstone to the instruction that has preceded it. Moreover, Jesus has just talked about his triumph, his victory over the world; and the same triumph is reflected in this prayer. Far from being gloomy and morose, the prayer adopts a long-range view which expects ultimate victory even while presupposing conflict.

To look towards heaven while praying was perhaps the most common posture at the time (cf. 11:41; Mark 7:34;

contrast the tax collector who 'would not even look up to heaven', Luke 18:13). Alternatively, a person might prostrate himself in prayer that was intense or anguished – a posture adopted by Jesus himself only a short time later, according to Matthew 26:39. In any case, the posture of the spirit and of the heart are more important than the posture of the body and of the limbs.

Jesus prays for himself (17:1–5)

Themes are so intertwined in this prayer that it is sometimes difficult to draw out a coherent outline; but we may usefully distinguish between the burden of Jesus' prayer for himself, and the rationale he offers for it.

1. The burden of the prayer. In a word, Jesus prays for glory: 'Father, the time has come. Glorify your Son, that your Son may glorify you . . . And now, Father, glorify me in your presence with the glory I had with you before the world began' (17:1*b*,5).

The time has come, the hour has come: Jesus has been speaking of this hour again and again, and at last it is upon him. It is the hour of his death on the cross, of his burial in the tomb of Joseph of Arimathea, of his three-day silence, of his triumphant resurrection, of his ascension to his Father in dramatic exoneration. The time has come; and Jesus prays that the Father might glorify his Son.

A little earlier, Jesus, anticipating the cross/resurrection/exaltation, said, 'The hour has come for the Son of Man to be glorified. I tell you the truth, unless an ear of wheat falls to the ground and dies, it remains only a single seed. But if it dies, it produces many seeds' (12:23–24). Here the glorification of the Son is unambiguously associated with his death. In 17:5, however, the glorification of the Son is associated with returning to the glory of his Father's presence: 'glorify me in your presence with the glory I had with you before the world began.'

Both aspects contribute to Jesus' glory. Jesus prays for glory, both the glory connected with the cross and the glory connected with the exaltation. The first connection is the more striking of the two. To men of Jesus' day, the Roman cross was a symbol of violence, torture and evil; to Jesus, it is the means of glory. It becomes the visible presentation of the redeeming love of God and of his Christ, the superlative manifestation of God's powerful, saving action on our behalf.

In one sense, of course, the fourth Gospel makes it clear that Jesus exhibited his glory throughout his ministry. The incarnation itself performs this function, for the apostle John comments, 'The Word became flesh and lived for a while among us. *We have seen his glory . . .*' (1:14). The miracle at Cana is understood to reveal Jesus' glory (2:11), as is also the raising of Lazarus (11:4,40). But the supreme revelation of the Father's glory through Jesus is the cross/resurrection/exaltation.

This supreme glory is linked with the glory Jesus shared with his Father before the world began (17:5). This is an unambiguous reference to Jesus' pre-existence (cf. also 1:1; 8:58; 16:28). But more, it signals a further link: the manifestation of the glory of God – this triune God of whom so much has been said in John 14 to 16 – reaches its apex not in a blinding flash of resplendent light, but in the agony and triumph of the cross and empty tomb. The glory of the cross is of a piece with the pre-existent glory of Jesus, which is itself of a piece with the glory he shares with his Father in triumphant declaration that his mission has been accomplished.

It must be carefully noticed, however, that the two verses (17:1,5) do not provide us with a mere *description*, but with a *prayer*. Jesus *prays* for the Father to glorify him. This means the Son prays that the Father will so accept his Son's willing and obedient suffering as by that suffering both to declare his grace to men and to restore his Son to his pre-incarnate glory. The thought is staggering.

If Jesus prays that the Father may glorify him, it must be noted that he prays this prayer in order that by his own glorification he may in turn glorify his Father (17:1). It will bring no glory to the Father if Jesus' sacrifice on the cross is not acceptable, or if the Son is not restored to his rightful place in the presence of the Father's unshielded glory. That would mean the divine mission had failed, the purposes of grace for ever defeated. For Jesus to pray in this way is therefore in essence for him to pray, 'Your will be done on earth as it is in heaven.' If the mission is to succeed, if Jesus is glorified both in the cross itself and in the exaltation which testifies that Jesus' obedient sacrifice is accepted, glory will accrue to the Father whose express will is thereby being accomplished. This point is spelt out clearly in verses 2–4.

2. The rationale Jesus presents to his Father. Part of the rationale for Jesus' prayer that he be glorified is enunciated in the prayer itself. As we have just seen, Jesus prays to be glorified in order that he may in turn glorify the Father. This ultimate purpose functions as a rationale for his own glorification.

This point is formalized in 17:2. Jesus prays for glory for himself, in order that he himself may glorify the Father (17:1); and then he adds, 'For you granted him authority over all people that he might give eternal life to all those you have given him' (17:2). The preposition translated 'for' in the NIV could well be rendered 'just as'. In other words, some correspondence is set up between 17:1 and 17:2.

17:1*b*	17:2
Statement (imperative): Glorify your son	*Statement:* You granted him authority over all people

JUST AS

| *Purpose:* That your son may glorify you | *Purpose:* That he might give eternal life to those you have given him |

Even a cursory reading of these two verses shows that they are not precisely parallel. Reading across, it appears at first glance that 'Glorify your Son' is scarcely the same thing as 'you granted him authority over all people'; and 'that your Son may glorify you' does not mean the same thing as 'that he might give eternal life to those you have given him'. Nevertheless, there is some legitimate connection, as the preposition translated 'for' (NIV) or 'just as' makes clear. Precisely what is that connection?

The answer to this question is best understood once we have come to grips with the nature of the authority the Father has given to the Son. 'You granted him authority over all people' (17:2*a*), Jesus says to his Father; but when was this authority granted, and what is distinctive about it?

Some have argued that the Father in eternity past gave authority to the Son to empower him for the work of the incarnation. However, Jesus does not exercise any such authority over all people during the days of his flesh. Others suggest that this gift of authority is a temporal act that belongs to the very nature of the Godhead: i.e., the Father serves as the *fons divinitatis*, the source of deity, in the eternal generation of the Son. This suggestion, however, reads the text anachronistically, finding elements in the New Testament which do not demonstrably belong there but which spring from debate of a much later period.

There is a better way to understand this passage. When Jesus says, 'For you granted him *authority over all people*,' he is referring to a decision in eternity past to grant Jesus authority over all people on the basis of his obedient humiliation, suffering, death, resurrection, ascension and exaltation. The thought is akin to Philippians 2:5–11: Jesus became obedient to death – even death on a cross; and 'therefore God exalted him to the highest place and gave him the name that is above *every name*, that at the name of Jesus *every knee* should bow, in heaven and on earth and under the earth, and *every tongue* confess that Jesus Christ is Lord, to the glory of God the Father' (Phil. 2:9–11). The decision was made in eternity past: on this basis Jesus can say, 'you *granted* [past tense] him authority,' just as Jesus can refer to those to whom he gives eternal life as those whom the Father *has given* him. The authority over all people was promised in the past and, because with God alone the decision and the doing are coextensive, the gift is as good as given from that point on. Nevertheless, Jesus actually receives this particular gift only after his cross-work and exaltation. Hence, in Matthew's Gospel, on the threshold of his ascension he declares, 'All authority in heaven and on earth has been given to me' (Matt. 28:18).

The purpose for this gift of authority is clearly stated. The Father granted Christ authority over all people in order 'that he might give eternal life to all those you [the Father] have given him' (17:2). The gift of eternal life depends on the cross/resurrection/exaltation of Jesus. Were there no cross-work, no resurrection, no exaltation, then sin could not be forgiven; for the Lamb of God would not have removed it. Jesus would not then have been the first person with a glorious new resurrection body: who then could have been thus transformed? The blessed Paraclete could not have been sent to convict the world of its sin, its righteousness and its judgment, or to generate new life in believers. The great commission would have lost not only its meaning but its basis: *all authority given to Jesus* is its foundation (Matt. 28:18–20). The reason why Jesus is granted this sweeping authority over all people is that he may have eternal life to all those the Father has given him.

This I take to be the correct interpretation of 17:2. We must therefore return to the question raised earlier: What is the nature of the connection between 17:1*b* and 17:2? The answer is reasonably clear. In 17:1*b* Jesus prays for what, according to 17:2, has already been given to him in principle. 'Glorify your Son,' he prays: that is, accept my obedient suffering and return me via the cross to the radiance of your unshielded presence – *just as* 'you granted him authority over all people': that is, just as you have already promised this exalted state. Moreover, the purpose of the Son's glorification (17:1*b*) is that the Father be glorified; the purpose of the gift of authority over all people (17:2) is that he might give eternal life to all those the Father has given him. *These two purposes are congruent.* As the Father is glorified before men, the people he has given to the Son come to true faith and eternal life; and conversely, as those the Father has given to the Son are brought to eternal life, the Father himself is glorified.

It appears, then, that verse 2 is related to verse 1*b* as the ground of a request is related to the request itself. Jesus prays, in effect, 'Father, you know that in principle you have given me a supreme position over all people, a position I am to receive as a function of my obedience unto death. You know that this position of authority was assigned me in order that I might give eternal life to all those you have given me. Now, Father, the time for these great events is here. My prayer, therefore, is that you fulfil your Word. Glorify your Son (just as you promised you would), in order that by bringing glory to you he might effect the salvation of those you have given him.'

Only this understanding of the relationship between verses 1*b* and 2 makes adequate sense of verse 3. Most commentaries treat 17:3 as a mere excursus, that because mention is made in 17:2 of 'eternal life', Jesus in 17:3 goes off on a short reflection concerning the essence of eternal life. If, however, verses 1*b* and 2 are linked to each other in the way I have suggested, then verse 3 is also integrally related to the context.

To grasp how this is so, we must first remind ourselves how important the knowledge of God really is in the Scriptures. According to the prophet Hosea, God's people are destroyed from lack of knowledge (Hos. 4:6). Conversely, the prophets can look forward to a time of unqualified blessing in these terms: 'For the earth will be filled with the knowledge of the glory of the LORD, as the waters cover the sea' (Hab. 2:14). An integral part of the new covenant is that all of God's people will know him, from the least of them to the greatest (Jer. 31:34; cf. Heb. 8:11). 'This is eternal life,' Jesus says, praying to his Father: 'that they may know you, the only true God, and Jesus Christ, whom you have sent' (17:3). No other definition is needed. Eternal life is best seen not as everlasting life but as knowledge of the Everlasting One. To know God transforms a person and introduces him to a life he could not otherwise experience. Knowledge of God is eternal life; to know God is to have eternal life.

Of course, this God whom to know is eternal life must be the God who truly exists, the true God, the only God. Our text makes this plain. Eternal life is to know 'the only true God' (17:3). It is not possible to choose any old god: only the knowledge of the true God is eternal life. Similarly, it is not possible to choose the way we shall know him: only the way he has defined is acceptable, that is, knowing Jesus Christ, whom he has sent (17:3).

The way in which men come to have eternal life is by coming to know God by coming to know Jesus. That is the point of 17:3. The reason the Son is given authority over all people is in order that he may give eternal life to all whom the Father has given him. That is the point of 17:2. It follows, then, that for the Son to fulfil the purpose of his mission, he must bring people to know God by bringing people to know himself. In other words, he must make God's glory visible to the people his Father has given him.

In one sense, of course, that is what Jesus has been doing all along. That is the purpose of the incarnation: 'The Word became flesh and lived for a while among us. *We have seen his glory . . .*' (1:14). 'No-one has ever seen God, but God the only Son, who is at the Father's side, has made him known' (1:18). Throughout his earthly ministry Jesus was revealing his Father's glory so that people might believe; for in revealing his own glory (e.g. 2:11) he was simultaneously revealing his Father's glory. That is why Jesus now prays, 'I have brought you glory on earth by completing the work you gave me to do' (17:4). For Jesus to say that he has completed (*teleiōsas*) the work the Father has given him to do (17:4) looks back on the sustained earthly ministry of revealing his

Father. But the greatest revelation of glory is still to come.

It is at the cross that Jesus supremely reveals his glory and makes known his Father. Above all else, the cross most dramatically and unambiguously unveils the glory of God. It is the cross which most clearly makes the Father and the Son known. A few short hours later, at the point of death, Jesus would be heard to declare, 'It is finished (*tetelestai*)' (19:30). With this climactic revelation of glory still ahead of him, Jesus asks his Father to glorify the Son in the impending death/resurrection/exaltation, in order that the Son may glorify the Father (17:1); for this glorification corresponds to what the Father has already granted the Son in principle for the express purpose of providing eternal life to those given him by the Father (17:2). In other words, by the glorification of the Father and the Son in the 'lifting up' about to take place, *the Father and the Son are most clearly made known*; and where they are truly known, there also is eternal life (17:3). Thus the glorification of the Son in this great redemptive event is itself the means of effecting the goal of the Son's mission, the granting of life to those who have been given into the Son's hand.

The argument, like the statement of the Counsellor's work in 16:7–11, is extremely compressed; but its main lines are clear. It follows, then, that Jesus is praying for himself in a very special sense; and only with careful qualification is it at all adequate to summarize this section (17:1–5) with the caption, 'Jesus prays for himself.' Perhaps we most easily glimpse its peculiarity when we contrast Jesus' prayer for himself with our prayers for ourselves. We are inclined to pray for ourselves in several distinct areas. For example, we pray about our external problems, real or imagined – our health, our social and vocational difficulties, our financial pressures.

Again, we pray about our sins: that is, we pray for personal holiness, for more instant obedience, for deeper faith and selfless love. Yet again, we pray for wisdom to discern the truth or to come to a sound decision on some issue or set of alternatives.

All such prayers for self enjoy some biblical warrant; but not one of them truly corresponds to the prayer Jesus offers for himself. Nowhere does Jesus in these verses mention any of his 'problems' or the decisions he must make. He offers no petition for improved health or the removal of social difficulties. And needless to say, the perfect Saviour offers no prayer for self-improvement or for the grace to abandon some self-acknowledged sin (cf. 8:46).

The essence of Jesus' prayer is that the Father's pledged will be done in his life, in order that God might be truly known and that thereby eternal life might come to men. When he prays, 'Glorify your Son,' he is not in some self-centred fashion clutching for honour as men count honour. Far from it; for the entire context militates against such an interpretation. After all, he is asking only for that which was his in eternity past (17:5), and which he temporarily abandoned in order to take on his saving mission. Moreover, the glory he seeks is by way of the cross; and it has as its purpose the glorification of the Father and the conversion of men. Besides, Jesus is asking for something already granted in principle to him by the decree of the Father. That is why Jesus could say on another occasion, 'I am not seeking glory for myself; but there is one who seeks it, and he is the judge' (8:50).

In short, Jesus prays that the Father's will be done on earth as it is in heaven. He prays for himself in exactly the same way he prays in Gethsemane (as recorded in the Synoptics), 'Not what I will, *but what you will*' (Mark 14:36; cf. Matt. 26:39; Luke 22:42), save only that his hesitation and fear have not yet surfaced in the personal agony vividly portrayed by the other Evangelists. (This, of course, can scarcely be used as an argument against John's historical credibility, since the Synoptists themselves indicate that Jesus was in full control of himself during the Last Supper. It is not until Gethsemane that Jesus begins to face his blackest hour concerning his Father's will.)

Jesus' prayer for himself is not intended to be taken primarily as a paradigm for our prayers. Perhaps the closest we may come to patterning our prayers for ourselves after the one Jesus offers for himself is to cry to God with all sincerity and no reservation that his will be fully accomplished in our lives. Such a prayer can be costly: in the extreme case it may lead to a martyr's crown. Alternatively, it may press us towards difficult service unrecognized by peers, or to quiet acceptance of personal pain and suffering. But it always leads to the best way that any person can possibly take; for God's way is the only way that enjoys his approval and blessing, and therefore bears ultimate significance.

Jesus prays for his followers (17:6–19)

This long central section of the Final Prayer opens with a brief review of the work which Jesus has already carried on, the work which (he has just noted) now stands complete (17:4). But we may consider the same verses from a slightly different perspective.

1. A brief review of who his followers are (17:6–10). Before offering specific petitions for his followers, Jesus identifies them by outlining several features which establish their place in God's redemptive purposes.

They have grasped the revelation of the Father in the Son. Jesus says, 'I have revealed you [lit., your name] to those whom you gave me out of the world. They were yours; you gave them to me and they have obeyed your word. Now they know that everything you have given me comes from you. For I gave them the words you gave me and they accepted them. They knew with certainty that I came from you, and they believed that you sent me' (17:6–8).

Jesus did not come simply to offer a high moral example. He came to give the words that God had given him (17:8; cf. 7:16; 12:48). It follows, therefore, that in receiving the words of Jesus, the disciples have received the words of God. That, of course, is just what Jesus intended: his purpose was to reveal God's name to those given him – to make known God's revealed character and essential nature. He came to make God known, a fact which both the prologue (1:18) and the words immediately preceding this prayer (17:1–5) make clear. And 'now' (17:7), at the end of the ministry, the disciples have come to recognize that everything Jesus has given them is indeed from God.[9] They may not yet enjoy massive comprehension and profound faith, but at least Jesus can say that the disciples have come to know 'with certainty that I came from you, and they believed that you sent me' (17:8). The disciples have grasped the essential revelation of the Father in the Son.

Even before Jesus' mission, the disciples were God's; and God gave them to Jesus. The point is repeatedly made. Jesus says that he revealed his Father 'to those whom you gave me out of the world' (17:6); and then he adds, 'They were yours; you gave them to me . . .' (17:6). The disciples belonged to God from the beginning inasmuch as he predestined them as his children. This thought is often repeated in John's Gospel (17:2; 6:37,44,65; and see on 15:16, chapter 5 of this book). It is a healthy antidote to human arrogance, which all too rarely recognizes the unbounded nature of divine sovereignty.

Christians often think of Jesus as God's gift to us; we rarely think of ourselves as God's gift to Jesus. The two gifts are not parallel: God's gift of Jesus to us is for the good of the recipients and the glory of the donor, whereas God's gift of us to Jesus is for the good of the gift (much as giving an orphaned child to adoptive parents is primarily for the good of the 'gift') and the glory of the recipient. We do nothing to earn God's gift of Jesus; Jesus paid everything to receive God's gift of us. Because God is God, he has both the right and the power to present a gift of certain blessed individuals to his Son; and the knowledge that he has done so is a tremendous incentive to evangelism. We may be assured that, if the Father has 'many people' (Acts 18:10), even if they have not yet come to the truth, they cannot but do so ultimately, or else the designation makes no sense.

The disciples have obeyed Jesus' word (17:6). Notwithstanding the predestinatory note just sounded, it must not be thought that the disciples are mere robots or puppets. They believe, they hear, they obey; and the belief is their belief, the hearing their hearing, the obeying their obeying. It is not easy to see how God's unconditioned sovereignty, even in salvation, and man's free agency as a creature in God's universe, can coexist; but coexist they do, according to the Scriptures. In expressing these truths, it is essential to avoid formulations in which God's activity and man's activity become mutually self-limiting. The Scriptures avoid such traps. Of the many stunning examples, perhaps none is clearer than Philippians 2:12–13: 'Therefore, my dear friends, as you have always obeyed . . . continue to work out your salvation with fear and trembling, for it is God who works

in you to will and to act according to his good purpose.'
Rightly construed, God's sovereignty in these matters
serves as an incentive to obedience and a spur to growth,
rather than as a stifling, fatalistic disincentive. So here in
Jesus' Final Prayer: the text leaps from the Father's predestinatory work to the disciples' obedience with neither
impropriety nor embarrassment.[10]

Some find great difficulty with the description of the
disciples, at this early stage, as people who have obeyed
God's word. It is argued that the description simply
does not fit the facts. The statement could only be true
years after this prayer, when the disciples have proved
themselves to be faithful witnesses during the early
years (and perhaps decades) of the primitive church. It
follows, then (so the argument runs), that Jesus could
not have prayed these words, or anything like them, at
this point in history. They must spring from the
Evangelist John who anachronistically inserts them into
the flow of the passage, making the disciples look better
than they are at the time of the passion by describing
their conduct at a much later period.

There are two factors which invalidate this interpretation. The first is that any person who was as clumsy an
editor as seems to be suggested by this theory could
scarcely have given us the literary masterpiece of the
fourth Gospel. Most of the verses in John 17 place both
Jesus and his disciples just before the cross, with little sign
of anachronism and many believable historical touches.
The prayer persistently mentions Jesus' imminent departure, refers obliquely to the disciples' uncertainty, fear and
the danger of defection. None of these features (with the
possible exception of the last) characterizes the church in
any early decade after Pentecost. To insert a reference to
the later church into this flow would signal remarkable
literary incompetence.

There is a second and more important factor. Close examination of the clause 'they have obeyed your word' (17:6) shows it is not anachronistic, nor is it an inaccurate description of the disciples during that last, fateful night. In John's Gospel keeping Jesus' *words* or God's *words* (plural) suggests observing all the divine precepts, instruction and commands; whereas obeying the divine *word* (singular) means, for the disciples, adhering in general to the gospel proclaimed by Jesus, without further entailment. The belief and obedience of the disciples is still shockingly immature. This is made clear, for example, by the exchange towards the end of the last chapter (cf. especially 16:31). But even there, as we saw, the disciples' faith is real, though it is indeed shallow. Others, after all, have long since abandoned Jesus (6:61–66), and one of the apostles, Judas Iscariot, has finally and decisively quit the band in order to betray the Master; but the others with Jesus on the memorable evening believe, at least, that Jesus came from God (16:30). And that is about all that is required of the words, 'they have obeyed your word' (17:6). Their faith and obedience, though still weak, fickle and immature, are nonetheless real; and Jesus, true to his word, takes care not to break the bruised reed nor extinguish the smoking wick.

The disciples are to be distinguished from the world. True, they once belonged to the world; but Jesus chose them *out of the world* (15:19) – or, otherwise put, the Father gave them to Jesus *out of the world* (17:6). Then, almost as if to make the distinction as unambiguous as possible, Jesus says, 'I pray for them. I am not praying for the world, but for those you have given me, for they are yours. All I have is yours, and all you have is mine' (17:9– 10*a*).

There are two opposite errors to avoid in coming to grips with this passage. The first error is to suppose that

because Jesus here prays exclusively for his disciples he
therefore has no concern for the world. This is denied a
little further on in this same chapter: we learn that Jesus
prays for his followers so that they may function as witnesses to the world, 'that the world may believe that you
have sent me' (17:21; cf. 17:18,23). The fact of the matter
is that Jesus must have some concern for the world or he
would not be found praying for his followers to bear
appropriate witness to the world.

The second error to avoid is to suppose that Jesus is
not praying for his disciples in any *exclusive* sense. Jesus
quite candidly says, 'I pray for them. I am not praying
for the world' (17:9). Of course, Jesus could not possibly
be praying for the world in the same way that he is praying for his disciples. He could not pray that the world
may be one, or that the world may be protected from the
evil one; for in the Johannine vocabulary 'world' is set
against God. The only thing that Jesus could be praying
with respect to the world is precisely that the world
cease to be the world. Otherwise put, Jesus later prays
for those who, though now in the world, will later
believe and thereby cease to be the world, but join with
his disciples.

There is a special kinship between Jesus and his disciples; and he offers special prayers for them, precisely
because they are God's (17:9). Appeal is thus again made
to predestination; and the same point is reiterated in the
next verse: 'All I have is yours, and all you have is mine'
(17:10*a*).[11] These words ground Jesus' special prayer for
his disciples in the fact that the Father's ownership of
the disciples is equally Jesus' ownership of the disciples.
Jesus prays for them out of his concern and love for
what is his own, assured at the same time that this
prayer for them cannot go unheeded since they belong
equally to the one to whom he is praying. Implicitly, of

course, these words also constitute a Christological statement of immense significance. Any mere mortal can pray to God, 'All I have is yours'; but no mere mortal can pray, 'All you have is mine.'

Would to God that the truths of these verses might burn themselves into our memories. It is a rare and holy privilege to observe the divine Son of God not only formulating his prayers but formulating the *grounds* for his petitions. These grounds reflect the essential unity of Father and Son, and reveal that Jesus' prayers for his people trace their argument back to the inscrutable purposes of Deity. When the Son of God himself has offered prayers for his followers like these prayers, and when the prayers have been grounded as these prayers have been grounded, it is horrifying to remember that, in moments of weakness and doubt, we still rebelliously question the love of God for his own people. This passage ought rather to engender the deepest and most stable faith, the most adoring gratitude. The disciples of Jesus Christ are loved with a special love (cf. also on 14:16–21, chapter 3 of this book) which distinguishes them from the world.

The disciples constitute a means of bringing glory to Jesus, who explicitly affirms, 'glory has come to me through them' (17:10*b*). As in the clause, 'Father, the time has come' (17:1), the verb is probably proleptic. Perhaps even during his ministry Jesus has been glorified by the degree of obedience and trust they have exercised towards him; but the arrival of the hour signals new triumphs. Christians glorify Jesus by their confession, their joyful obedience, their mushrooming faith, their willingness to suffer and serve.

In these points, then, Jesus briefly summarizes who his disciples are before he offers petitions to his heavenly Father on their behalf.

2. Jesus prays for the protection of his followers (17:11–12,14–15). There appear to be two elements.

First, Jesus prays that the disciples may be protected from disunity. 'I will remain in the world no longer, but they are still in the world,' Jesus says; and then he refers to the impending cross/resurrection/exaltation in the familiar terms, 'and I am coming to you. Holy Father, protect them by the power of your name – the name you gave me – so that they may be one as we are one' (17:11).

Jesus prays that the disciples may 'be one'. In Greek, this quite clearly does not mean 'become one', but simply 'be one'. The idea is not that they may progressively achieve unity, but simply that they may be a unity continually.

It is crucial to the understanding of this petition to note that Jesus does not simply request unity for his followers, but rather requests his Father to grant protection to his followers so that they may be unified. The implication seems to be that various dark forces will strive to break up this unity; and nothing less than the power of the Father's name – that is, the revealed character of God - is adequate for the task of protection. During Jesus' mission, he kept his followers safe by the name – the revealed character of God – given him: 'While I was with them, I protected them and kept them safe by that name you gave me' (17:12*a*). However, now that Jesus is leaving the earth, he requests his Father to take over this responsibility.

Should anyone mention that one of the Twelve fell away, suggesting thereby that Jesus' power to protect his own was fatally flawed, Jesus has an answer: he reports that, as a result of his protection, 'None has been lost except the one doomed to destruction so that Scripture would be fulfilled' (17:12*b*). It follows that the Father's will – that Christ preserve those given him (6:38ff.) –was therefore perfectly carried out; for Judas turns out not to be a genuine exception, but one who, through his own treachery and evil, fulfilled the Scripture and thereby also stood within the divine will.

The constant goal is that the disciples be one as Jesus and his Father are one. Like any analogy, this cannot legitimately be pressed without limit. The unity enjoyed by Jesus and his Father has numerous features which could not be duplicated in the unity among believers. For instance, Jesus and his Father are but two; the believers are many. Jesus and his Father stand together in their creative work (1:1–3); this cannot be predicated of the disciples. Jesus and his Father enjoyed the brilliance of pre-temporal glory (17:5); but obviously that unity could not in the nature of the case be shared by temporal creatures. Many other such distinctions suggest themselves on the basis of the fourth Gospel alone.

Yet clearly the analogy is important, and must not be robbed of all content by endlessly peeling the onion. Many of the relational ties between Jesus and his Father described by John's Gospel are functional in nature. Moreover, as chapter 2 of this book demonstrated, if Jesus stands with his Father with respect to man in revelation and authority, he simultaneously stands with man with respect to his Father in dependence and obedience. Within this framework, the Father and the Son enjoy a perfect unity of love, of purpose, of holiness and of truth. Now, Jesus prays, so protect these people you have given me that they may be one as we are one: one in love (a theme already stressed, 13:34–35; 15:13), one in purpose (obedience, fruit-bearing, witness – all prevalent themes in these chapters), one in holiness (it is not for nothing that Jesus here addresses his Father as 'Holy Father', and will shortly ask him to sanctify the believers), one in truth (they, unlike the world, have come to recognize the fundamental truth that Jesus is the revelation of God).

This theme of unity is an important one in Jesus' prayer. It is picked up again and repeated (17:21,22,23), and so we shall return to it in the last chapter of this book – at which time its relevance to the modern church may be usefully explored. For the moment, it may be helpful to note that, if the prayer is a request that Jesus' disciples be protected in order that they may be one in love, purpose, holiness and truth, it follows that the greatest dangers lie in those things which seek to destroy unity in love, in purpose, in holiness and in truth.

An adequate catalogue of such evils, coupled with a careful assessment of their danger, would immediately double the length of this book. Such a catalogue would include jealousy, hate, friction, arrogant isolationism, selfishness, bitterness, an unforgiving spirit, a wretched tongue; for these vices seek to destroy the unity of love. The catalogue would go on to mention one-upmanship, an uncooperative spirit, brinkmanship and impatience (which threaten unity of purpose), all kinds of sin (which abhors holiness), and lies, dogmatic half-truths, unwillingness to admit error or sympathetically to learn from one another, chronic unbelief (which all conspire to obliterate unity in truth). From all such evils, good Lord, deliver us.

If Jesus thought it necessary to pray for this kind of unity for his followers, how much more should we deem it necessary to pray in this way for ourselves? 'How good and pleasant it is when brothers live together in unity! . . . For there the LORD bestows his blessing, even life for evermore' (Ps. 133:1,3). So writes the psalmist; and most believers can testify to the holy power and joy that turn on such unity.

Second, Jesus prays that the disciples may be protected from the evil one. 'I have given them your word and the world has hated them, for they are not of the world any more than I am of the world. My prayer is not that you take them out of the world but that you protect them from the evil one. They are not of the world, even as I am not of it' (17:14–16). The evil one, apparently, often operates through the hatred of the world (cf. 15:18 – 16:4); and the disciples are going to need protection against such malice. After all, they are going to remain in the world after Jesus leaves; yet, because they have been chosen out of the world and have been born again by the Spirit's unobserved action (John 3), they no longer belong to the world. Henceforth the world no more determines their distinctives than it determines Christ's. True to form, the world therefore hates them (cf. 15:18ff. and chapter 6 of this book).

Even though they face such evil, the Christians are not to seek escape from the world by death or by hermitage. Jesus makes explicit that his prayer is not that the disciples should be removed from the conflict. Nor, in the light of 16:1–4, is Jesus asking that his followers be spared all pain and suffering that might erupt from the world's implacable hatred. Rather, he prays that his people might be spared from the evil one, even when they find themselves facing the world's opposition. Persecution is one thing; persecution without defence against the dark attacks of the evil one on mind and spirit is another thing. Jesus prays for protection against the latter.

Many years later John remembered the Master's prayer and, observing those around him, testified that young men in his own day were still overcoming the evil one (1 John 2:13–14). He insisted that the one who is truly born of God cannot be touched by the evil one (1 John 5:18).

The spiritual dimensions to this prayer of Jesus are consistent and overwhelming. By contrast, we spend much more time today praying about our health, our projects, our decisions, our finances, our family, and even our games, than we do praying about the danger of the evil one. Materialists at heart, we often discern only very, very dimly the spiritual struggle of which Paul (for instance) was so deeply aware (Eph. 6:10ff.). The Lord's (model) prayer likewise teaches us to pray, 'Deliver us from the evil one' (most likely the correct rendering). Certainly the church will not produce many spiritual giants when it fails to discern its chief enemy.

In short, Jesus prays for the protection of his followers – protection from disunity, which in most instances would be prompted by their own sin, and protection from the devil himself, the external source of some temptations and opposition.

3. A further purpose to Jesus' prayer. 'I am coming to you now,' Jesus tells his Father, still speaking proleptically, 'but I say these things while I am still in the world, so that they may have the full measure of my joy within them' (17:13).

It is not entirely clear whether 'these things' refers to all of John 14 to 17 or only to the prayer of John 17. The latter is perhaps marginally more likely. If so, then Jesus is saying 'these things', that is, he is praying this prayer, before he returns to his Father by way of the cross, so that his followers may one day have the fullest joy. Their joy will be greater for remembering that Jesus, on the night he was betrayed, prayed for his followers. When in the future they recognize that his requests on their behalf are being fulfilled in their lives, they will be especially grateful and full of joyful hope as they recall this prayer.

This interpretation of the passage suggests that although Jesus is praying to his Father, he is praying to be heard by his disciples. He did this on more than one occasion. At the tomb of Lazarus he prayed, 'Father, I thank you that you have heard me. I knew that you always hear me, *but I said this for the benefit of the people standing here, that they may believe that you sent me'* (11:41–42).

No doubt private, secret prayer is to be more important to us than public prayer (Matt. 6:5–6); but in the Scriptures there is also a place for public, corporate prayer. At such times, it is only right that the one praying should remember the others who are listening to his prayers, even if his prayer is not directed towards them. More preparatory thought expended before prayer meetings and other occasions when public prayer is appropriate would enhance the legitimate, public aspects of such prayer. There is little place for spiritual narcissism or for a long list of purely private matters, or for pious but inaudible mumbling when the church gathers together to pray.

4. *Jesus prays for the sanctification of his followers.* 'Sanctify them by the truth; your word is truth' (17:17). To be sanctified is to be set aside for God and his purposes; and here Jesus prays that God may sanctify – i.e., set apart for his own use – the believers. The means for such sanctification is the truth, God's Word.

It is difficult to see how there could be much genuine sanctification apart from such a means. As men absorb increasing quantities of God's Word, cherishing it because it is true, they become set aside for God's purposes. After all, what a man thinks is what he is; therefore perpetual reflection on God's Word inevitably makes a man truly God's. And sanctification is not merely Jesus' will for the Eleven; it is God's will that all of his people should be holy, sanctified (1 Thess. 4:3).

Contextually speaking, the sanctification in question is not only to personal holiness, as important as that is. That purpose of God for which these first believers are especially set aside is expressed in the next verse: 'As you sent me into the world, I have sent them into the world' (17:18). Jesus had to set himself apart for this mission to come into the world; he had to set himself to do his Father's will. In short, he had to sanctify himself. But that mission is now reaching its apex: viz. the cross, always the cross. And so Jesus resolves afresh to do the Father's will; but he recognizes that his own 'sanctification' to perform the will of the Father by going to the cross is somewhat different from the disciples' sanctification. His own sanctification is not a step which makes him holier, but rather one which establishes the basis for his disciples' sanctification: 'For them I sanctify myself,' he prays, 'that they too may be truly sanctified' (17:19); and their sanctification has as its goal witness to the world. Moreover, even if his apostles are primarily in view (in light of 17:20), nevertheless it applies to all believers inasmuch as Jesus prays that all of them may have an impact on the world (17:21–23).

It appears, then, that Jesus sets himself apart to perform his redemptive work on the cross, in order that the beneficiaries of that work might set themselves apart to the work of mission. Jesus would remind them, after his resurrection, that the sanctification he prayed for them was not meant to have merely personal, pietistic ends in view. Far from it: 'As the Father has sent me, I am sending you' (20:21).

> So send I you to labor unrewarded,
> To serve unpaid, unloved, unsought, unknown,
> To bear rebuke, to suffer scorn and scoffing –
> So send I you to toil for Me alone.
>
> So send I you to bind the bruised and broken,
> O'er wand'ring souls to work, to weep, to wake,

To bear the burdens of a world aweary –
So send I you to suffer for My sake.

So send I you to loneliness and longing,
With heart a-hung'ring for the loved and known,
Forsaking home and kindred, friend and dear one –
So send I you to know My love alone.

So send I you to hearts made hard by hatred,
To eyes made blind because they will not see,
To spend, though it be blood, to spend and spare not –
So send I you to taste of Calvary.

E. Margaret Clarkeson (1915–2008)[12]

Yet let it be said without hesitation that the note struck in this prayer is not gloomy. Like the earlier warnings about persecution (15:17 – 16:4), the purpose is not to engender gloom, but rather realism mingled with triumphant faith. If Jesus' prayer for our sanctification entails mission into the hating world, that mission becomes real joy to us simply because it is the Father's will; for, as with Jesus himself (15:11), our joy springs from doing God's will.

Jesus Prays for All Believers and for the World

'My prayer is not for them alone. I pray also for those
who will believe in me through their message, that all of
them may be one, Father, just as you are in me and I am
in you. May they also be in us so that the world may
believe that you have sent me. I have given them the
glory that you gave me, that they may be one as we are
one: I in them and you in me. May they be brought to
complete unity to let the world know that you sent me
and have loved them even as you have loved me.

'Father, I want those you have given me to be with me
where I am, and to see my glory, the glory you have given
me because you loved me before the creation of the world.

'Righteous Father, though the world does not know you,
I know you, and they know that you have sent me. I
have made you known to them, and will continue to
make you known in order that the love you have for me
may be in them and that I myself may be in them.'

Strictly interpreted, Jesus' prayer for his followers in
the preceding verses (17:6–19, chapter 9 of this book) is

concerned only with those who were already established as his disciples on that last, fateful night. True, many of the elements of that prayer apply equally to later believers; and indeed some of its ingredients are repeated in the verses now before us, which record Jesus' prayer for those who would later become his disciples. But in the strictest sense, the section 17:6–19 has horizons which need expanding; and 17:20-26 serves this purpose. 'My prayer is not for them [his immediate disciples] alone,' Jesus says. 'I pray also for those who will believe in me through their message' (17:20).

The fact that Jesus can proceed to this next step argues strongly that he foresees a period during which witnesses will spread the wonderful truth of the gospel. One is reminded of Jesus' words, 'And this gospel of the kingdom will be preached in the whole world as a testimony to all nations, and then the end will come' (Matt. 24:14), or of Jesus' decisive declaration, 'I will build my church, and the gates of Hades will not overcome it' (Matt. 16:18). Jesus foresees a continuing community of believers on the other side of the cross. In short, Jesus expects to leave his disciples behind to constitute his church.

The fact that Jesus looks to the future and perceives this expanding circle of witnesses dominates 17:20–23. Even when he prays for their unity, he looks beyond their unity to the still unconverted world which stands in need of the witness generated by that unity. In this way these verses develop the theme of witness to the world through the sanctification of believers, a theme already introduced in the immediately preceding verses (17:16–19).

It must not be thought that, with so much interest on a continuing group of believers, there is no place left for future eschatology. Jesus also prays for ultimate blessing for his disciples: the ineffable privilege of beholding the glorified Jesus in his exalted state (17:24). After reaching such breathless heights, the prayer then ends with a survey of Jesus' ministry, past and future (17:25–26).

Jesus prays for the unity of all who will become his disciples (17:20–23)

The paragraph before us (17:20–23) is tightly interwoven; but we may delineate its central themes under three headings.

1. The expanding unity. Already in praying for his current disciples, Jesus has prayed that they might be one (17:11). This unity for which Jesus prays is now developed in two ways. First, Jesus insists that this unity is one which includes 'those who will believe' through the message of the existing disciples (17:20). He prays 'that all of them may be one, Father, just as you are in me and I am in you' (17:21).

In terms of the unity of the church, the apostles do not enjoy any special advantage. The believer in the twentieth century is to belong to the unity of this body as much as the first believers; for so Jesus prays. It follows that the unity with which Jesus is concerned is an expanding unity, not a static one. The thought is staggering: men and women from various races, cultures, languages and value systems become believers in Jesus Christ and as a result become incorporated into this expanding unity for which Jesus prays.

This unity theme is developed in a second way. It is qualified a little further to enable us to glimpse more accurately the nature of the oneness. Referring to the multiplying converts who will constitute this unity, Jesus prays, 'I have given them the glory that you gave

me, that they may be one as we are one: I in them and
you in me' (17:22–23a); or again, 'May they also be in us
. . .' (17:21). What do these words mean?

We may begin by asking this question: If Jesus can say,
'I have given them the glory that you gave me,' then what
is the nature of the glory which the Father gave the Son?
The answer to that question is straightforward: the glory
the Father gave the Son was the glory of the humility of
the incarnation, culminating both in the glorification
of the Son at the crucifixion and in the glory of his resurrected and exalted state. Believers have seen something of
this glory, except for the glory Christ now enjoys; and
that, too, they shall one day see, since Jesus prays to that
end (17:24).

But the words 'I have given them the glory that you
gave me' are ambiguous, and may say more than I have
suggested so far. They may indicate not only that Christ
has given us his glory, in the sense that we can now perceive it, but also that Christ has given us his glory in the
sense that we now possess it. If the latter thought is
included, the text is telling us that our true glory is the
way of the cross. That way is vindicated by the glory of
triumph later; but already we have something of Jesus'
glory inasmuch as we, like him, are to endure the enmity
of the world and walk as suffering servants. This is our
glory, not our shame. W. Barclay comments, 'We must
never think of our cross as our penalty; we must think of
it as our glory . . . The harder the task we give a student,
or a craftsman, or a surgeon, the more we honour him
. . . So when it is hard to be a Christian, we must regard it
as our glory, as our honour given to us by God.'

The unity among true believers is not only likened to
the unity that exists between Jesus and his Father
(17:22), a point made earlier (17:11) and already shown
to be a unity of love, of purpose, of holiness and of truth,

but it is also a unity which turns on mutual indwelling. Jesus prays that all of them may be one, 'just as you are in me and I am in you. . . . I in them and you in me' (17:21,23). Indeed, Jesus goes farther yet and prays, 'May they be brought to complete unity . . .' (17:23), suggesting now that the unity is to grow and be perfected.

The analogy between the unity of believers and the unity enjoyed by Jesus and his Father is coherent only if the functional aspects of the Christology of John's Gospel (outlined in chapter 2 of this book) are kept in mind. We have seen that it is the Father, living in Jesus, who performs Jesus' works (14:10). Although the Son is in the Father, coeternal with him in the unity of the Godhead, yet he is dependent upon him and obedient to him in the self-emptying of his mission. The Father and the Son, though one, remain distinct. In a similar way, the Father and the Son, by means of the promised Counsellor, live in the disciples (14:23) so that the disciples, like Jesus, become the sphere of divine activity (14:12). As they remain in the vine, they bear fruit (15:1ff.). This comes about as they stand in dependence upon (15:4) and obedience towards (15:10–11) the one who lives within them.

The unity to be enjoyed by Christ's disciples is a unity based on a mutual indwelling: the indwelling of the Spirit in each of them, and their living in God – dependent upon him, relying upon him, obedient to him, maintaining the sacred gospel entrusted to them and by which they are saved. This is at once the experience and the commitment of every true believer.

Like sanctification, this oneness is simultaneously something already achieved and something that needs perfecting. On the one hand believers, if they are true believers, are already one: the triune God has already taken up residence within them, and they live by faith in

Jesus Christ. This is common for all of them. Theirs is a common experience of grace, a common object of faith, a common eternal destination, a common regeneracy, a common rejection of the 'world', a common perception of the Lord's glory. These ties make them one. The things that unite true Christians are so deep and eternal that they transcend the things that divide them. Christians are truly one.

On the other hand, Christians need to grow in their unity; for Jesus prays, 'May they be brought to complete unity . . .' (17:23). The implication is that their unity, while real, is not perfect. Sad to tell, too often Christians do not cherish deeply the things that unite them with other true believers: they cherish instead the divisive things. Even where there is some point of conscience at stake, there is a danger that in defending what we hold to be a point of truth we may endanger the integrity of this witness of loving unity. At the level of praxis, at the level of attitude, at the level of love, at the level of a growing grasp of true doctrine – at all of these levels the Christian church needs to be perfected in unity. For this Jesus himself prays; and one day he will see this prayer answered without qualification. The expanding unity will yet become the perfect unity.

2. The multiplying witness. The unity for which Jesus prays has a further end in view. Jesus prays for this unity 'so that the world may believe that you have sent me' (17:21). He adds, 'May they be brought to complete unity to let the world know that you sent me and have loved them even as you have loved me' (17:23).

The expanding unity generates a multiplying witness: that is how the church grows. The first disciples told the message, and others came to faith (17:20). The enlarged circle witnesses and loves, and still others believe. The

world itself is the constant target; and as men and
women in the world confront the witness of the church,
some at least come to recognize that God sent his Son
and loves his people in the same measure that he loves
his Son (17:23).

The multiplying witness of the church has two elements to it, according to this passage. The first is proclamation of the message (17:20) which is to be believed
(17:20–21,23). The second is the public demonstration of
the unity for which Jesus prays (17:21,23), calling to
mind the purpose of the 'new commandment': 'All men
will know that you are my disciples if you love one
another' (13:35). Both aspects of our witness are essential. The truth of the gospel, announced without the
demonstration of the power of the gospel in transformed
and loving lives, is arid. It may be beautiful in the way
that the bad lands can be beautiful; but not much grows
there. On the other hand, the demonstration of love
within a believing community does not by itself proclaim the source or cause of that love. Attractive in its
own right, like a luxuriant South Sea island, nevertheless such love does not call forth disciplined obedience
or informed belief, and cannot of itself call others to true
faith. It is merely a place to rest. The multiplying witness
Jesus has in mind is both prepositional and exemplary,
both confessional and demonstrative. It is a witness of
word and of love.

3. *The revealed Christ.* This theme, the theme of Christ
being revealed, is subtly interwoven into the fabric of
this passage. At the centre of the expanding unity, as the
subject-matter of the multiplying witness, Jesus is being
unveiled to a lost world. He is the content of the message to be revealed; and his is the glory that is given to
the disciples. Above all, he is the revelation of the Father,

so that, if the disciples witness as they should, what the world comes to know (Jesus tells his Father) is 'that you sent me and have loved them [the disciples] even as you have loved me' (17:23). The disciples' unity in love is so unearthly that only the truth of Christ is adequate to explain it.

Thus, although Christians witness propositionally, they are not merely outlining a system of interrelated truths but they are pointing to Christ; and although they manifest unity in love, purpose, holiness and truth, that very unity testifies to the divine love, which not only stands behind them but is supremely set forth in the sending of Christ. Christ stands at the centre; and it is Christ who is revealed in the church's witness.

Best of all is the fact that the ultimate reward for the church is the ultimate revelation of Christ's glory (17:24). Before going on to explore this truth, however, we might profitably reflect a little on the way the theme of unity in John 17 is sometimes used in modern ecclesiastical circles.

To some people, the term *ecumenism* has only good connotations. Utter the word, and they hear harps playing and angels singing; or if harps and angels are deemed too ethereal, at very least a certain fire lights up their eye. To others the same word evokes only images of evil. Ecumenism is intrinsically a doctrine of compromise which emasculates the gospel and wickedly flirts with apostasy and assorted forms of unbelief. The first group tends to cite John 17 in its favour; the second group tends either to ignore John 17 or else to include within the unity only a very small group, while denying the unity in such innocuous terms (e.g., making it entirely a positional unity with no entailment for conduct) that it becomes difficult to see how such unity could ever serve as a witness of anything to the world. What does the text say?

The text refers to a unity of all true believers. The unity in question, as we have seen, is partly a function of being disciples of Jesus Christ, and partly something towards which we must grow and in which we must be perfected. This unity is not *merely* positional, for it is to function as a witness before the watching world; indeed, one might argue that it is *the* characteristic mark of the believing community.

On the other hand, we cannot help but observe that organizational unity is simply not in view. This is not to say that the unity for which Jesus prays could not issue in organizational oneness; but it is to say that organizational oneness is not fundamental or essential. The outward manifestation of this spiritual unity is not a neat organizational flow-chart, but a compelling witness.

The problem is compounded today by the fact that Christendom uses the word *Christian* or the expression 'disciples of Christ' in highly diverse ways. For some, a Christian is a person who believes in a supreme being vaguely associated with the Christian heritage. For others, a Christian is a moralist of sorts. Still others want the term to refer to everyone who has been baptized (by whatever mode and at whatever age) in the name of the Father, Son and Holy Spirit. Yet again, others use the word to refer to those who claim to have been 'born again' (whatever that means to them), or who have 'accepted Christ as Saviour' (which is not a New Testament category). How can 'Christian unity' refer to something unambiguous, when the term *Christian* means anything we want it to mean?

This is not the place to work out an essential set of beliefs and practices necessary to justify the appropriation of the word *Christian*. However, if the term is to have anything like its New Testament meaning, then for a person to be a Christian he cannot legitimately hold to a belief structure which the New Testament explicitly disallows, or adopt practices which the New Testament explicitly forbids. More positively, he must at very least hold to what the New Testament itself insists is a minimum confession or an essential practice. If he does not, he prostitutes the term *Christian*.

Let us come to cases. Suppose someone confesses, 'Jesus is Lord' (cf. 1 Cor. 12:3). Does this guarantee that the person in question is a Christian? Regretfully, no. In the Corinthian situation, of course, the test of this confession was both a necessary and a sufficient criterion. There was very little dispute regarding who Jesus really was; and truly to confess this Jesus as Lord, in the midst of a polytheistic society where such an exclusivistic claim stood out, was unambiguously the work of the Holy Spirit. Today, however, the question of who Jesus is cannot be thought of as a given.

To the classic liberal Jesus is the greatest moralist. To confess him as Lord means nothing more than to agree to follow high moral standards. To the Bultmannian, very little can be affirmed regarding the historical Jesus. To confess this Jesus as Lord is not to do more than open oneself to the possibility of authentic existence. For others, Jesus is both God and man, but his sacrifice on the cross was not a sufficient atonement for our sins: there must be additional sacrifice and penance. For such a person to confess 'Jesus is Lord' may be to pass this confessional criterion with respect to Jesus' *person*, while nevertheless falling under the curse of another criterion which lays down limiting beliefs concerning Jesus' *work* (e.g. Gal. 1:8–9). Another person may confess 'Jesus is Lord' to indicate his formal agreement with the tenets of orthodoxy (just as a person may recite superficially the Apostles' Creed), yet fail to acknowledge Jesus' Lordship over his ethical practices, including both his private but consistently selfish conduct and his business practices. Such a person passes the test of I Corinthians 12:3 from a merely doctrinal perspective; but, failing to submit to the implications of lordship, he may fall under the searching tests of moral obedience and growing love (see, for instance, 1 John). In each of these instances, the confession 'Jesus is Lord' serves as a *necessary* but not a *sufficient* criterion for being a genuine believer, a disciple of Christ, a Christian.

It does not take much knowledge of the current ecclesiastical and theological scene to recognize that, if basic New Testament tests are preserved and applied to the sweep of modern Christendom, not everything that calls itself *Christian* truly qualifies. Charitable as we may wish to be, that person is not Christian (in any New Testament sense) who steps unambiguously beyond the bounds of what the Scriptures recognize to be a true believer in and disciple of Jesus Christ – the Jesus Christ who has revealed himself in history and who is revealed in the pages of the holy Scriptures.

This should not be thought surprising. After all, when Jesus came into the world and expounded the nature of God to his own race, only a remnant of his people perceived who he was. Judaism made many claims and reflected highly diverse belief structures; but not all Jews who expounded Judaism espoused Christ. Only a remnant came to faith in Christ. So, too, with Christendom: there are many belief structures and competing ethical and theological norms, but not everyone in 'Christianity' (broadly conceived) espouses the Christ who has revealed himself to us. There will always be tares sown along with the wheat; and the final separation awaits God's timing. Meanwhile we are very foolish or very naive if we think there is no difference between weed and wheat.

If these reflections have any validity, they may prove helpful when we try to assess the ecumenical movement. If ecumenists seek to join together into one organization all branches of 'churchianity' known to Christendom, then they are trying to unite wheat and tares. Even if we acknowledge that every church has some true believers within it (and I am not certain that is so), the systematic denial of biblically required truth or the wholesale disregard for biblically mandated conduct in certain groups does not inspire confidence. John 17 does not look to a unity made up of both believers and members of the 'world'. Anyone who is not a true believer constitutes part of that world which stands in antithetical relation to the unity of the church. Whoever cites John 17 to justify a unity that embraces believer and apostate, disciple and renegade, regenerate and unregenerate, abuses this passage. Such ecumenism has its roots not in Scripture but in misguided (if well-intentioned) notions of what New Testament Christianity is all about.

On the other hand, the things which tie together true believers are far more significant than the things which divide them. The divisive things are not necessarily unimportant: sometimes they are points of faith or practice which have long-range effects on the church for good or ill, reflecting perhaps some major inconsistency or misapprehension concerning the truth. Nevertheless the things which tie us together are of even more fundamental importance. Regardless of denominational affiliation, there ought to be among Christ's people a sincere kinship, a mutual love, a common commitment, a deep desire to learn from one another and to come, if at all possible, to a shared understanding of the truth on any point. Such unity ought to be so transparent and compelling that others are attracted to it. To such biblical ecumenism (if I may so label it) there is no proper objection. Indeed, it is mandated by the Final Prayer of the Lord Jesus himself.

Jesus prays that his disciples might enjoy the ultimate blessing (17:24)

'Father, I want those you have given me to be with me where I am, and to see my glory, the glory you have given me because you loved me before the creation of the world' (17:24).

1. The content of that blessing. In a word, the content of that blessing is Jesus Christ himself, visible in unshielded glory. Jesus looks ahead to the end of the age. The disciples cannot follow him 'now' (13:33,36): indeed, Jesus makes clear he is not asking the Father to take them out of the world (17:15). But the time is coming when that will change. After all, Jesus has already promised to come back and take the disciples to be with him (14:3). The same perspective is now presented again: Jesus wants those given to him to be with him where he is, and to see his glory – that is, his glory within the Godhead, the glory that is his inasmuch as he is God.

This cannot fail to stir the Christian. Theologians refer to this ultimate bliss as the *visio Dei*: the vision of God. Without it, heaven would be an empty triumph; with it, the venue is unimportant.

> Face to face with Christ, my Savior,
>   Fact to face – what will it be
> When with rapture I behold Him,
>   Jesus Christ who died for me?

> Only faintly now I see Him,
>   With the darkling veil between;
> But a blessed day is coming
>   When His glory shall be seen.
>
> *Mrs Frank A. Breck (1855–1934)*

The glory of Christ is the more wonderful precisely because it is twofold. He chose to walk among us with a rather paradoxical glory of humiliation, in order to save us and raise us to heaven's heights, enabling us to see the unqualified brilliance of the divine glory rightfully his.

> Thou who art God beyond all praising,
>   All for love's sake becamest Man;
> Stooping so low, but sinners raising
>   Heavenwards by Thine eternal plan.
> Thou who art God beyond all praising,
>   All for love's sake becamest Man.
>
> *Frank Houghton (1894–1972)*

2. The Godhead's love as foundation of that blessing. Verse 24 reminds us that the Lord Jesus is central to this final blessing. It is his glory which is seen. But his glory depends on the love relationship within the triune God. Jesus' glory, he tells his Father, is 'the glory you have given me because you loved me before the creation of the world' (17:24). C.K. Barrett comments, 'The ultimate root of the final hope of men lies in the love of the Father for the Son, that is, in the eternal relationship of love which is thus seen to be of the essence of the Holy Trinity.' This loving relationship extends from eternity to eternity, from 'before the creation of the world' to the consummation when Jesus' glory will be fully revealed to his own people, those the Father has given to him.

Jesus surveys his ministry (17:25–26)

In these final two verses of John 17 Jesus surveys his ministry towards those the Father has given him; and he focuses attention not only on his past ministry but also on his future ministry.

As far as the past is concerned, he prays, 'Righteous Father, though the world does not know you, I know you, and they know that you have sent me. *I have made you known to them*' (17:25–26a). Jesus stands in contrast to the world: the world does not know God, and did not recognize Christ (1:10), but Christ himself knows God fully. Christ has therefore performed a mediatorial function and made God known to those given him; and these have come to know that in truth he was sent from God. Jesus' knowledge of God is immediate; theirs is mediated through Jesus.

Not only does Jesus say that he has made God known throughout the period of his ministry which is now drawing to a close, but he goes on to say, 'and [I] *will continue to make you known* in order that the love you have for me may be in them and that I myself may be in them' (17:26). This continued work will be by means of the promised Holy Spirit. By this continued ministry, the love of the Father for the Son will extend to the disciples and fill them, and Jesus himself will be present in them by the agency of the Counsellor (cf. 14:23). Jesus' departure does not have as its goal the abandonment of the disciples to solitary isolation. Far from it: his goal is to sweep up those the Father has given him into the richness of the love that exists among the Persons of the triune God. At the same time he lives in and among his own redeemed people through the agency of the Holy Spirit, whom he bequeaths.

No more we doubt Thee, glorious Prince of life;
Life is naught without Thee: aid us in our strife;
Make us more than conquerors, through Thy deathless
    love;
Bring us safe through Jordan to Thy home above.

Esmond Louis Budry (1854–1932)
tr. Richard Birch Hoyle (1875–1939)

Endnotes

[1] I have discussed this question in some detail in my book *Divine Sovereignty and Human Responsibility: Some Aspects of Johannine Theology against Jewish Background* (London: Marshall, Morgan and Scott, 1980). What I have written above is a simplification of a few of the themes treated with a little more rigour in the other volume.

[2] Cf. also Acts 10:41: 'He was not seen [after the resurrection] by all the people, but by witnesses whom God had already chosen – by us who ate and drank with him after he rose from the dead.' Many take the promise in John to refer to the disciples' ability to 'see' Jesus by means of the Spirit after the Spirit has been sent, not as a reference to Jesus' resurrection appearances. The arguments are complex on both sides, and for the sake of brevity I omit them. On balance, however, it seems there is far too great a tendency among modern commentators to reduce both the resurrection appearances and the parousia to the ministry of the Paraclete. As far as the resurrection appearances are concerned, John goes to considerable pains to detail a representative collection of them; so it is scarcely conceivable that none of the promises in the Farewell Discourse that speak of seeing Jesus again refers to seeing the resurrected Christ.

³ Because 18:1 says that 'Jesus *left* with his disciples and crossed the Kidron Valley', many have argued that he and his followers could not have *left* the upstairs room until then. If so, then 14:31 can scarcely be taken in the way I have suggested. However, the verb used in Greek is not always to be taken so strongly. Although it commonly means 'to go out' or 'to leave', it sometimes has the weaker force of 'to go' or perhaps 'to go forth' or 'to go forward'. Just a few verses on, in 18:4, the same verb appears in this weakened sense: 'Jesus, knowing all that was going to happen to him, *went out* and asked them, "Who is it you want?"' At this point Jesus is clearly outside, and so is the approaching crowd. Jesus does not 'go out' in any literal sense; rather, he 'goes forward'. The same sort of usage may occur in 18:1.

⁴ For further exploration of this theme in John's Gospel, see my *Divine Sovereignty and Human Responsibility: Some Aspects of Johannine Theology* (London: Marshall, Morgan and Scott; Atlanta: John Knox, 1980).

⁵ There is an extremely difficult textual choice to be made at this point, between the future indicative *genesesthe* and the aorist subjective *genesthe*. Syntactically, the former can on rare occasions take on the meaning of the latter in this construction. Whatever the reading, the text is not telling us that fruit-bearing makes a person a disciple, but that fruit-bearing is the necessary and visible sign that one is in truth a disciple. The NIV rendering, though paraphrastic, is certainly correct.

⁶ See footnote 4 above.

⁷ See D.A. Carson, 'The Function of the Paraclete in John 16:7–11', *Journal of Biblical Literature* 98 (1979), pp. 547–566.

⁸ Others argue that the verb should not be rendered *convicts* at all; but I am persuaded that it is by far the best option in this context. For a detailed defence of this position, see the article cited in the preceding footnote.

[9] It might have been less confusing if 17:7 had said, 'Now they know that everything I have comes from you' instead of the tautologous 'Now they know that everything you have given me comes from you'. But the latter phraseology stresses Jesus' dependence on his Father, a major theme in John's Gospel (see chapter 2 of this book).

[10] I have discussed this question elsewhere, at a rather more strenuous level – see chapter 5.

[11] In Greek the 'all' is neuter plural, instead of masculine (as might be expected when referring to persons). When John elsewhere refers to the elect in the neuter gender, he normally employs the singular. The neuter plural expression in this verse is designed to be all-embracing: that all of the elect belong to both Father and Son is grounded in the greater fact that *everything* the Father has belongs to the Son, and vice versa.

[12] Copyright 1954, 1966 by Singspiration, Inc. All rights reserved. Used by permission.

New Carson Series from Authentic

Released Summer 2010, individually or as a boxed set

978-1-85078-892-8

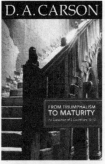

978-1-85078-890-4

978-1-85078-889-8

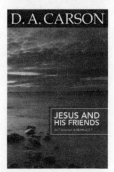

978-1-85078-891-1

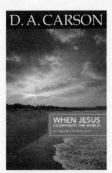

978-1-85078-890-4